Samuel Macauley Jackson

The Laws of Trade

as adopted by the Board of trade, the Union stock yards and transit company the

Lumberman's exchange and the Produce exchange of the city of Chicago together

with some practical hints in shipping

Samuel Macauley Jackson

The Laws of Trade
as adopted by the Board of trade, the Union stock yards and transit company the Lumberman's exchange and the Produce exchange of the city of Chicago together with some practical hints in shipping

ISBN/EAN: 9783337187026

Printed in Europe, USA, Canada, Australia, Japan

Cover: Foto ©Suzi / pixelio.de

More available books at **www.hansebooks.com**

JOSLIN'S RE-SAWING MACHINE.

Weight of Machine, 3,500 Pounds. Price, $1,200.

61 S. Canal St.,
CHICAGO.

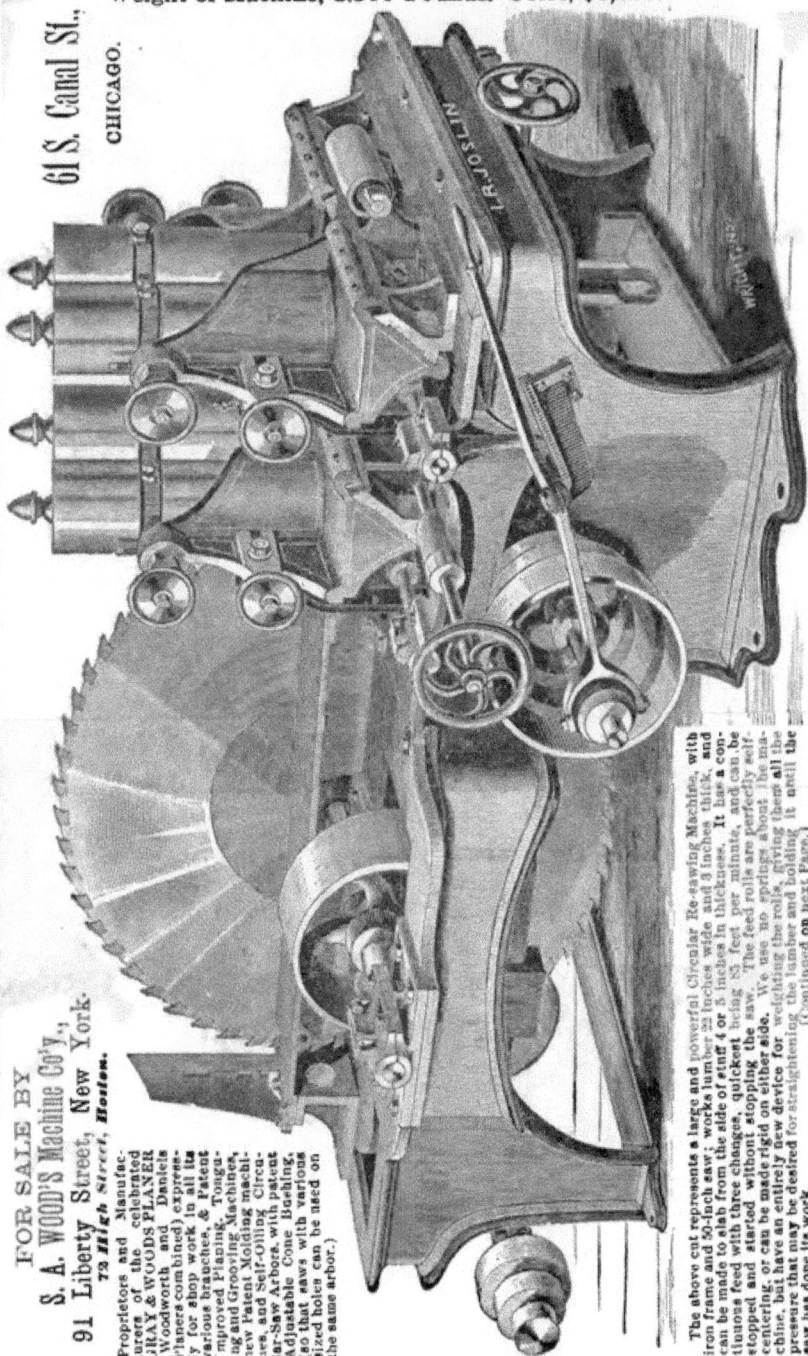

The above cut represents a large and powerful Circular Re-sawing Machine, with iron frame and 50-inch saw; works lumber 22 inches wide and 3 inches thick, and can be made to slab from the side of stuff 4 or 5 inches in thickness. It has a continuous feed with three changes, quickest being 33 feet per minute, and can be stopped and started without stopping the saw. The feed rolls are perfectly self-centering, or can be made rigid on either side. We use no springs about the machine, but have an entirely new device for weighting the rolls, giving them all the pressure that may be desired for straightening the lumber and holding it until the saw has done its work. [Continued on next Page.]

As can be seen by the cut, we run the saw close up between the rolls. We hold the lumber so firm and rigid that we are able to make six pieces from an inch board. The whole feed-works are moved across the machine by the hand-wheel on the side, if desired to slab from the side of stuff and use the self-centering arrangement. The manner in which we connect our roll-stands to the sides, allows them to work perfectly free at all times, and with all our improvements combined, we claim to be able to do a larger variety of work with our Re-Sawing Machine than can be done with any other, and one-third more in the same time. Another very important point we claim for our machine, is that any man can run it who can file and keep a saw in good order. We have several of these machines in operation, which give the very best satisfaction, and we are prepared to put them in on trial. Parties ordering machines will please state what kind of work they are required to do; if picture-back work altogether, sawed from thick lumber, we can give a saw with the machine adapted to that class of work—lighter guage. Our regular guage will take less than ¼ inch kerf.

Driving pulley on saw 18 in. diameter, 9 in. face, and should run 650 revolutions per minute. We can furnish counter-shaft when desired with these machines.

BILLIARD

ESTABLISHED 1855.

———— ◆◆◆ ————

George M. How & Co.

COMMISSION MERCHANTS,

FOR THE PURCHASE AND SALE OF

Grain, Provisions, Seeds, &c

153 Monroe Street,

CHICAGO.

Prompt Personal attention given to all business entrusted to our care.

CORRESPONDENCE SOLICITED.

CHARLES J. GILBERT.   CHARLES W. BREGA

GILBERT & BREGA,

Commission Merchants,

Grain, Provisions & Seeds,

163 Washington Street,

CHICAGO.

CORRESPONDENCE SOLICITED.

CHICAGO
BURLINGTON & QUINCY
RAILROAD.

SHIPPERS OF LIVE STOCK,

FROM

MISSOURI, KANSAS, INDIAN TERRITORY, NEW MEXICO,
TEXAS, IOWA AND NEBRASKA.

Should bear in mind that the Route, via.

C. B. & Q. R. R.

Affords Greater Facilities for the Safe and Quick Transportation of Live Stock,

Than are offered by any other line.

THE COMPANY'S NEW & COMMODIOUS FEEDING YARDS

At Quincy and Galesburg, Illinois,

And at Creston and Burlington, Iowa,

Enable Drovers to feed, water and rest their Stock, then, after a SHORT RUN, to
unload their Cattle or Hogs at the

UNION STOCK YARDS IN CHICAGO.

In good condition for Market.

Drovers' Cars fitted with Sleeping Berths for the comfort and convenience of men
in charge of Stock, are attached to all Stock Trains.

C. W. Smith, Traffic Manager, Chicago.   G. L. Carmon, Div Fr't Ag't, Rock Island, Ill.
E. P. Ripley, Gen. Fr't Ag't, Chicago.   Thos. Miller,   "   Burlington, Io.
Paul Morton, Ass't G. F. A.   "   R. M. Miles,   "   Quincy, Ill.
       Fred. Harvey, Gen'l Western Fr't Ag't, Leavenworth, Kansas.

LOCKLAND MILLS.   RIALTO MILLS.   CRESCENT MILLS.

Clarke, Friend, Fox & Co.

Manufacturers and Dealers in

PAPER

150 AND 152 CLARK STREET,

CHICAGO.

Louisiana Route.

Chicago and Kansas City

SHORT LINE,

—VIA—

CHICAGO & ALTON R. R.

—AND—

ST. LOUIS, KANSAS CITY AND NORTHERN R. R.

—AND—

Passing through MEXICO, Mo., LOUISIANA, Mo., JACKSONVILLE, BLOOM-
INGTON and NORMAL. At the latter point, 124 miles from CHICAGO,
are new and extensive STOCK YARDS, COVERING TWENTY
ACRES, thoroughly drained, and with clear spring water carried in pipes to every pen. Yards of equal extent have
also been built at Louisiana, 273 miles from Chicago, and 217 miles from Kansas City, making easy runs
for Stock, bringing it to market in as good condition as when
loaded at point of shipment.

LUXURIOUS DROVERS' SLEEPING CARS,

Fitted up with the comforts and conveniences of a Pullman Palace Car, attached
to Stock Trains on this favorite route. SLEEPING BERTHS FREE
to Drovers in Charge of Stock.

QUICK TIME.

Rates of Freight always as Low as by any other Route.

THE GREAT IRON BRIDGE AT LOUISIANA IS COMPLETED.

NO DRIVING OR FERRIES BY THIS LINE.

CHEAP FEED AND ABUNDANCE OF CLEAR WATER.

By this route, shippers from MISSOURI, TEXAS, KANSAS, the SOUTH-WEST,
St. Louis, Springfield, Jacksonville, and other points, are enabled to avail themselves of the CHICAGO MARKET, in transit to the East without additional cost.

J. C. McMULLEN,
General Manager, Chicago.

W. H. REED,
Gen. Western Agent, Kansas City.

R. P. TAUSER, Jr.,
Agent Kansas City.

JAMES SMITH,
Gen. Freight Agent, Chicago.

SAMUEL SMITH,
General Agent, St. Louis.

L. DYOWK,
Stock Agent, St. Louis.

UNION HORSE NAIL CO.

MANUFACTURERS OF THE

STAR HORSE NAILS,

OFFICE AND FACTORY,

ASHLAND AVE., NEAR 22 ST.,

CHICAGO.

Our Nails are made with

LARGE and SMALL HEADS

FROM THE BEST NORWAY IRON, AND ARE POINTED
FINISHED AND BLUED, READY FOR USE.

SEND FOR SAMPLE CARD.

SILVER MEDAL AWARDED AT ST. LOUIS FAIR, 1875

THE OLD CHAMBER OF COMMERCE.

DESTROYED BY FIRE OCTOBER 9TH, 1871.

THE NEW CHAMBER OF COMMERCE.

ERECTED 1872.

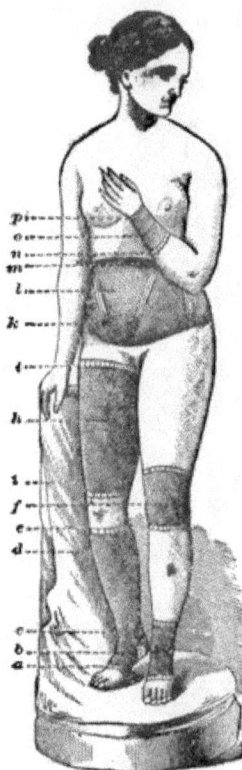

THE

LAWS OF TRADE,

AS ADOPTED BY THE BOARD OF TRADE, THE UNION STOCK YARDS AND
TRANSIT COMPANY, THE LUMBERMAN'S EXCHANGE AND THE
PRODUCE EXCHANGE OF THE CITY OF CHICAGO—TO-
GETHER WITH SOME PRACTICAL HINTS IN
SHIPPING &c., &c.

BY

SAMUEL JACKSON.

CHICAGO:
PITKIN & CRUVER, PRINTERS,
REAR 119 CLARK STREET.
1878.

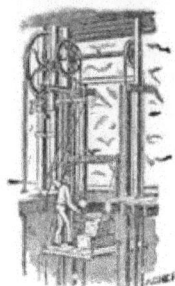

PREFACE.

The Compiler and Publisher of this work has been led so to do from the apprehension of the need of such a hand-book by the special branches of trade to which its pages are devoted, and the commercial community generally. He has been induced to undertake the task of its preparation at the suggestion and solicitation of prominent gentlemen connected with the several interests herein set forth, and has spared no pains to render the volume accurate in every particular, as well as of appreciable value as a convenient work of reference.

The title chosen for the compilation seems to the author to be both appropriate and comprehensive—"The Laws of Trade, as adopted by the Board of Trade, the Union Stock Yards and Transit Company, the Lumberman's Exchange, and the Produce Exchange." It has been the compiler's aim to collate every important fact and statistic, with reminiscences of early days, which should not be permitted to slumber in forgetfulness, relating to these very prominent business interests of Chicago and the Northwest; and in his labors to this end he has been ably and cheerfully aided by leading merchants in all the lines indicated, who have communicated much interesting and useful information on the subjects treated upon, for which favors he feels duly grateful.

The advantages of such a work as this are so apparent as to render quite unnecessary any extended elucidation thereof. While it cannot but prove in many ways of positive value to the local trade, it is likewise calculated to benefit producers and dealers throughout the West and Northwest, who will find in its pages such reliable information as will show them the best market for their products and the most favorable point at which to make their purchases. Some advertisements of first-class representative business houses appear herewith, to which the attention of the public is invited. They offer the best of inducements to the trade at large, and all having dealings with them have the assurance of the most satisfactory results accruing therefrom. With these brief introductory remarks, this volume is respectfully submitted to the mercantile and agricultural community, in the confident hope that it may meet the views and answer the requirements of all whom it may concern.

CONTENTS.

	Page
Chamber of Commerce,	1
Board of Trade,	1
Board of Trade—future deliveries,	24
Puts and calls,	29
Option trading,	32
Margins on time contracts,	36
Remarks concerning option trading,	37
Expenses—buying and shipping,	40
Legal opinion on option contracts,	41
The anti-corner rule,	55
Caution to short sellers,	59
Deals of the curbstone brokers,	64
Rules governing inspection of grain,	64
Weights,	69
Rates of inspection,	70
Weighmaster's tariff of prices,	70
Regulations governing the inspection of flour,	71
Regulations for the inspection of hay,	75
Regulations for the inspection of provisions,	76
Requirements as to cut and packing hog products,	78
Union Stock Yards and Transit Co.,	85
Union Stock Yard—How business is done there,	90
Receipts and sales of live stock,	96
Live stock commission merchants,	97
Packing houses,	100
Transit House,	103
* Union Stock Yards National Bank,	105
* Officers of the Lumberman's Exchange,	106
Receipts and shipment of lumber from 1847 to 1877, inclusive,	108
The Lumberman's Exchange and Lumber trade,	110
Lumber inspection,	113

CONTENTS

Go s & Phillips' Manufacturing Co., - - - - - 116
The officers of the Produce Exchange, - - - - - 119
The Produce Exchange, - - - - - - - 120
The Fruit and Berry Ordinance, - - - - - - 123
Game Laws of Illinois, - - - - - - - 126
Instructions for packing butter, - - - - - - 127
Advice to shippers of butter, - - - - - - 128
Roll butter, - - - - - - - - - 129
Tare on butter packages, - - - - - - - 130
Instructions to shippers, - - - - - - - 130
Game for shipment, - - - - - - - 131
How to kill and ship poultry, - - - - - - 131
To shippers of cheese, - - - - - - - 133
To shippers of vegetables, - - - - - - - 133
Instructions for preserving eggs, - - - - - - 133
Instructions for packing eggs, - - - - - - 135
What constitutes a car load, - - - - - - 137
Commission charges for selling, - - - - - - 138
Shipping perishable merchandise, - - - - - - 140
Decisions in admiralty, - - - - - - - 143

CHAMBER OF COMMERCE.

The stately, massive and beautiful Chamber of Commerce building, standing on the corner of Washington and La Salle streets, occupies the same site upon which was erected the structure that was dedicated to business purposes, with imposing and memorable ceremonies, on the 30th and 31st of August, 1865, and which was destroyed by fire in the great conflagration that raged with irresistible fury in the business center of Chicago in October, 1871; and with the energy and go-a-headitiveness, which are the characteristics of this people, the present magnificent building was completed and dedicated with appropriate and impressive ceremonies on the 9th day of October, 1872, just one year from the date of the destruction of the edifice formerly occupied by them and formally taken possession of by the commercial organization for whose use it was erected. The building is three stories in height, constructed in the most substantial manner of Ohio sand stone. In architectural style, it may be called the Composite, uniting the massive with the ornate. It has a frontage on Washington street of 93 feet by 181½ feet on La Salle street. The basement story is occupied by banking, insurance and commission houses and for other business purposes; the same may be said of the second story. On the third story, which is made accessible by broad iron stairways and a powerful elevator, are the exclusive apartments of the

BOARD OF TRADE.

The main room, or Exchange Hall, is 142 feet in length by 87 feet in width, with a ceiling 45 feet in height. The President's rostrum is situated at the north end, and at the south end, over the door of entrance, is the visitors' balcony. The ceiling and the walls are beautifully and

appropriately frescoed, making it the most imposing and elegant hall in
the country for the purposes for which it is designed. At the south end
of the floor, separate from the Exchange Hall, are situated the offices of
the Secretary and the rooms for committee purposes. The building is a
conspicuous ornament to the city, comparing favorably in its architectural
beauty and grandeur with the innumerable business palaces and other
magnificent structures for which Chicago is famous, while it reflects the
highest credit upon the organization to which it belongs. Within the
walls of this elegant structure the members of the Board of Trade
assemble in grand array for business purposes, "and to them as a body
of representative merchants, who have contributed in a greater measure
than any other, belongs the credit of giving to Chicago her world re-
nowned prestige for business sagacity, and of her being a driving, won-
derfully enterprising and energetic community;" and from the very in-
significant inception of this association in 1848, to which we refer elsewhere, it has become formidable in numbers and wields an influence second to no other organization in the country. Its membership has reached the large number of eighteen hundred and thirty-one names,
which is twelve less than there were one year ago. The cost of a membership is one thousand dollars and the dues throughout a year are about
twenty dollars—though the membership is transferable and is often
transferred when a member retires from the Board, or for other causes is
sold for a less amount. The amount of business transacted by
these merchants and speculators, is, as we might say, almost fabulous.
      Charles Randolph, Esq., the able and esteemed Secretary of the
Board, informs us that the actual receipts and shipments of merchandise
which passed through the Board, the past year, reached the vast amount
of two hundred and eighteen million dollars; but it should be remembered that to meet the demands of speculation, which is always rife during
'Change hours, that this same merchandise changes hands, how often it
would be difficult to determine. Here, in this vast assemblage, meeting
from day to day, are gathered, men of experience, ripe with intelligence,
keen-witted, well posted on all public affairs, constantly scanning the
political horizon of this country and Europe—quick to observe the smallest incident happening that may have the slightest influence upon the
market one way or the other, prepared at once to operate, and when the
opportune moment arrives to meet the views of one side and also the
other—the bulls and bears array themselves in factions, the one to sustain and the other to depress the market; contending with relentless

pertinacity, the one side holding the vantage ground for a time and then the other—and thus purchases are made enormous in amount and almost countless in numbers. Therefore, it can be readily observed how difficult it would be to reach any approximate idea of the amount of business transacted annually on the Board. But if it could be ascertained no doubt the figures would be so colossal as to excite our special wonder. As evidence of its importance and the great influence the Chicago Board of Trade has upon all the markets of the world, we quote an able writer, who says: "The movements of this Board have always been watched with interest throughout this country and Europe; its dicta, concerning markets, have swayed the commercial centers of the world. Depressions of its business, or occasional reverses met with in the vicissitudes of its transactions, have been felt at every mart of importance in existence." Such is a brief outline of this powerful organization, and well does it merit all that may be written in its behalf, for an abler body of merchants never assembled, and amid all the excitement incident to the large and numerous operations in which they engage during 'Change hours, their equanimity is never disturbed. Their good humor is proverbial. Even the oldest and most austere and dignified among them are unable to withstand the amusement afforded by the jokes and sports of which the younger members are always brimful and running over. And gathered here, there are many, very many noble and generous men who, burdened with the cares attendant upon constant strife with the business world, nevertheless are never so deeply oppressed that their manly and generous natures are not always alive for charitable deeds or any good work or philanthropic enterprise that may be presented. Let the appeal come from the North, the South, the East or the West, they willingly come forward and respond with a lordly and an unsparing hand, as if in emulation of the world's benevolence to Chicago when she laid prostrate from the visitation of the great conflagration of October, 1871. But as it is our purpose in this work to show the steady increase and marvelous growth of the commercial interests herein represented, by statistics and other facts; and as we have, in introducing our subject, briefly written of the Board of Trade of to-day, let us here retrace our steps and go back to the day when the sagacious merchants of that period foreseeing the future greatness of Chicago as a metropolitan commercial center, first laid the foundation of this potent regulator of the world's business pulse in breadstuffs and provisions.

In seeking, as we have, with earnest efforts to reach all or a great part of the facts which make the history of the early days of the Board of Trade, we have found it a difficult task, and there does not appear to be anything extant, better and fuller regarding those interesting events —without it may be the record of the Board now in the possession of Mr. Secretary Randolph—than the subjoined historical information which we extract from a speech delivered by the late Hon. W. F. Coolbaugh, on the occasion of the inauguration of the Chamber of Commerce building, October 9th, 1872. He said: "It appears that the first organization of the Board of Trade took place in 1848. On the 13th of March of that year a call was issued for a meeting of the business men of the city for the formation of a board. The call was signed by the following well known firms to-wit:

"Wadsworth, Dyer & Chapin; George Steele; I. Burch & Co.; Gurnee, Hayden & Co.; H. H. Mazie & Co.; Neff & Church; John H. Kinzie; Norton, Walker & Co.; DeWolf & Co.; Charles Walker; Thomas Hale; Thomas Richmond, and Raymond, Gibbs & Co.

"At that meeting the proper initiatory steps were taken by the adoption of resolutions recognizing the necessity for a Board of Trade, adopting a constitution, and appointing a committee to prepare by-laws. At a second meeting, on the first Monday in April, the report of this committee was adopted, and a general invitation extended to the merchants and business men to meet with the Board, daily, at their rooms, over George J. Harris' flour store, on South Water street, which they had rented for $110 per annum. George Smith, the great Scotch banker, was elected their First President, but declining to serve, Thomas Dyer was chosen in his stead, and Charles Walker (a name always mentioned with respect), and John P. Chaplin were elected First and Second Vice-Presidents. The directors chosen were G. S. Hubbard, E. S. Wadsworth, George Steele, Thomas Richmond, H. G. Loomis, John Rogers, George F. Foster, R. C. Bristol, J. H. Dunham, G. A. Gibbs, John H. Kinzie, C. Beers, W. S. Gurnee, J. H. Reed, E. K. Rogers, J. H. Burch, A. H. Burley, W. B. Ogden, O. Lunt, E. H. Hadduck and L. P. Hilliard. In the list of members we find the additional names of Matthew Laflin, Joseph T. Ryerson, M. C. Stearns, J. C. Walter, J. A. Smith, Julian S. Rumsey, John C. Haines, George M. Higginson and others then, as now, recognized among the most honored, respected citizens of Chicago. In April, 1849, the first annual meeting was held, and the officers re-elected, with John C. Dodge as Secretary. A committee was appointed to procure daily telegraphic reports of the Eastern markets for the use of the members. The

hour for daily meeting on 'Change was fixed at 9 A. M. The legislature having passed an act of incorporation the winter previous, in April, 1850, the old board went out of existence and a new one was organized under the law, with the following provisions: 'This organization shall be called the Board of Trade of Chicago. Annual and semi-annual meetings shall be held and special meetings shall be called at any time at the written request of any five members. Each member joining the association shall sign the constitution, and, with the exception of the old members, pay five dollars, and, in addition, pay such sums semi-annually as may be voted by the board.' The annual dues in addition to the fee for admission were, I believe, two dollars for each member. Shortly after this time the startling fact that there was a deficit of $146.20 in the treasury of the old Board was discovered. The annual dues were immediately raised from two to three dollars, and the old members joining the new Board were required to pay three dollars and thus this enormous debt which had created such consternation was honorably extinguished. In 1850 the principal proceedings of the board were the adoption of resolutions complimentary to Stephen A. Douglass and Gen. James Shields for their services in obtaining from Congress a grant of land to aid in the construction of the Illinois Central railroad. The daily meetings of the board were so thinly attended that it was hoped a different time of meeting would prove more acceptable, and the 'Change hour was fixed between 12 M. and 1 P. M. By the time of the annual meeting in 1851, the affairs of the Board had become decidedly blue. The treasurer's book showed a balance, on the wrong side, of $165.96 and no assets. Another assessment of $4 on the members was made, and the institution went on. Frequently during that year only one of the members would put in an appearance at the hour of meeting, and it is fair to suppose that the transactions of the Board were rather limited. There were probably no 'corners' then. Sometimes not even one member appeared. In 1852 the Board changed its location to the corner of South Water and Clark streets, where the fourth annual meeting was held. There were now fifty-three names on the roll of members. Another removal was made in that year to No. 8 Dearborn street, where the fifth annual meeting was held in 1853. The most important proceedings this year were the equalization of rates for the handling of goods, and the adoption of a resolution to found a bank with a capital of $5,000,000 for the convenience, of the commerce of Chicago. It was also resolved to appoint a committee to take soundings of the Chicago harbor, and petition the Common Council for an appropriation to defray the expenses of the same. It was still a matter of great difficulty to get members to attend, and at this time a happy thought struck one of the members. He proposed, and the proposition was instantly and unanimously adopted, that the Secretary be directed to furnish a free lunch consisting of crackers and cheese with a glass of ale for the members. From this time the attendance on the Board began to increase, and its fortunes to improve. It is a common saying, that the way to men's hearts lies through their pockets, but the Board of Trade, in 1853, improved on this adage by the discovery that the way to their brains and enterprise lies through their stomachs. In April, 1854, the sixth annual meeting was held; George L. Gibbs, President; W. D. Houghtelling, Vice-President; and James E. Dalliba, Secretary and Treasurer. The location of the Board was again changed, this time to the corner of Wells and South Water street (over Purinton and Scranton's store), where they paid $250 per year rent, and allowed W. D. Wilson the use of the rooms for taking care of them. The transactions of the board during this year began to increase in magnitude. In April, 1855, at the seventh annual meeting, Hiram Wheeler was elected President; S. B. Pomeroy, Vice-President; and W. W. Mitchell, Secretary. A reading room was this year established. The board now warmly interested itself in the Georgian Bay canal, and sent William Bross and George Steele to Canada to advocate it before the Canadian Government. It may be remarked in this connection that they were successful in getting a charter, and ground was afterward broken for the work, but beyond this nothing was done, and the thing was passed over and apparently forgotten. It appears that about this time the daily supply of crackers and ale was in some way neglected, and the attendance of members soon began to fall off and became 'small by degrees and beautifully less.' Then the supply was resumed, and then came a crowd of 'dead beats,' to keep out whom a door-keeper was appointed, and the Board again went on flourishingly. At the eighth annual meeting in April, 1856, forty-five new members were added, and now the Board was in a more flourishing condition than ever. Charles H. Walker was elected President, cards of admission were issued, a permanent door-keeper was appointed, and the daily attendance of members was so good that the refreshments were ordered discontinued. From this time onward, the prosperity of the Board was uninterrupted. The lower floor of Walter's building was rented for $1200 per annum, and the hour of daily meeting changed back to 9 A. M. As evidence of its prosperity, at

one time, on the 6th of October of this year, 122 new members were admitted. At the ninth annual meeting in 1857, seventy-three new members were received. The Board was now exceedingly prosperous. Mr.
P. L. Wells, formerly connected with 'The Press,' was appointed Superintendent, to look after its interests, with a salary of $1500 a year. At
the tenth annual meeting in 1858, twenty-nine new members were admitted. Julian S. Rumsey was elected President; F. H. Barber, Vice-
President, and W. W. Mitchell, Secretary. The admission of members
was now confined to actual residents. The offices of Secretary and Superintendent were consolidated. The Grain Inspector's duties were defined, and in October, Lee and Armstrong were given permission to dis-
pose of stocks twice a week at auction in the rooms of the company. A
new charter was obtained, conferring privileges commensurate with the
expanding growth of the commerce of the city, and this charter was,
with a new set of rules and regulations, presented to the Board and approved. At the time of the eleventh annual meeting in 1859, there were
520 members on the Secretary's list; and on the proposition of John S.
Newhouse, the Board resolved to lease for the year the second story of
a new building he was then erecting on South Water street, at $1,250
per annum. These rooms they took possession of in February, 1860,
and occupied until their removal, in 1865, into the magnificent hall
which stood where we now are until its destruction in the terrible conflagration of the 9th of October, 1871. In April, 1860, the 12th annual
meeting was held. There were now 625 members. Warehousemen
were now required to make weekly statements of grain in store, and
daily reports of shipments. In April, 1861, the thirteenth annual meeting was held. The roll now contained 725 members, and the treasurer
held in his hands a surplus of over $4,000. In this month the rebellion
broke out, and when the rebel flag was hoisted over Sumpter, the stars
and stripes were unfurled over the Board of Trade of Chicago.

"It would give me unspeakable pleasure to speak of the noble and pat-
riotic support which through the whole four years of civil war, distinguished your body in its devotion to the Union, but the history of the
part it bore in the bloody conflict needs no recital here. The records of
its deeds are known to the country, and are imperishable. From this
point in its progress the board rapidly grew in importance and influence,
and the magnitude of its transactions began to attract the attention of
the great commercial centers of the country. Its subsequent history is
so familiar to us all that I will not occupy your time with any detailed

account of its official acts. From the smallest beginnings it has become
one of great numerical strength, numbering now, I believe, over 1200
members, and recognized as one of the most powerful and influential
commercial organizations in the world. When the few public spirited
merchants whose names I have mentioned first assembled in that little
room on South Water street, twenty-four years ago, Chicago contained a
population of only 20,000. For years the annual transactions of the
Board amounted to a sum so paltry that it would hardly be sufficient to
run a modern 'corner' in anything for a week. The voluminous statistics prepared by your able and accomplished Secretary, and laid on your
tables each year, furnish an interesting study for the merchant and business man. In 1850, only twenty-two years ago, the entire shipments of
grain of all kinds from Chicago, amounted to just 1,276,593 bushels. For
the year 1872, they will exceed 80,000,000 bushels. In 1859, the shipments of corn were 262,013 bushels. In 1872, it is estimated they will
exceed 40,000,000 bushels. In the winter of 1851 and 1852 the number
of hogs packed was 22,036. During the last winter, immediately succeeding the great fire, which some of our neighboring cities supposed
had destroyed our commerce, the number had exceeded 1,200,000. In
1865, the total receipts of live hogs for the whole year were 757,072.
From the first of January to the first of October, 1872, the enormous
number of 2,136,244 hogs have been received in Chicago, an excess of
742,970 over the same period of 1871, and the cry is still they come.
During the same time, being the first nine months of this year, the number of cattle received was 522,435, an excess of 90,000 over the same
time in 1871. I have no official statistics of the receipts of the present
year of many other products of the country which seek a market here,
but I have no doubt they will show, in most cases, a corresponding increase. In 1860, the number of pounds of wool received here was 859,-
248. In 1871, there were received 27,026,621 pounds. In 1860, we received 262,000,000 feet of lumber. In 1871, over 1,000,000,000 feet.
But I will not weary you with these dry details. Familiar as they may
sound to you, these enormous figures amaze and excite the world. When
we bear in mind that the transactions of your Board are confined to the
staple products mainly of the West, and do not include any portion of
the general merchandize, foreign and domestic, sold in Chicago, the magnitude of the business done on the Board of Trade seems incredible. It
has been estimated that the trading done on 'Change the present year
(1872) amounts to at least $300,000,000."

These were the utterances of the late Mr. Coolbaugh on the auspicious occasion of the interesting ceremonies attendant upon the dedication of the new Chamber of Commerce building in 1872. And as he proceeds in his review of the many years that had intervened up to the time from the date in 1848 of the small gathering of merchants that met to take the initiatory steps, and records the many difficulties they encountered from year to year before the Board of Trade of Chicago could be regarded as being permanently established, his statements are full of interest and embody the early history of one of the most important and influential institutions of the Western Commercial Emporium. That it is destined to "grow with the growth and strengthen with the strength" of the great city of which it is the just pride, is beyond question.

At the annual meeting held in 1859, Julian S. Rumsey was re-elected President, and Thomas H. Beebee was elected first Vice-President, and Stephen Clary, Second Vice-President; Seth Catlin was elected Secretary and George Watson, Treasurer, which offices they held until 1862.

It was during Mr. Rumsey's administration that he urged upon the Board certain reforms, and in these matters was ably assisted by George M. How, Esq., and Charles E. Culver, Esq. And resulting from such action statistical reports were first established as well as inspection on grain, and the Board were now beginning to get into good shape and transactions were being placed upon a more equitable basis. Mr. Rumsey was one of the early actors in the work to establish the Board, and through a long and highly creditable business career, he has been active, and no other member of the Board has done more to promote its well doing.

In 1860, Ira Y. Munn was elected President; Eli Bates and John V. Farwell, respectively, first and second Vice-Presidents. Some idea of the growth of the Board up to this time, may be gained from the fact that the storage capacity of the elevators of the city was 6,815,000 bushels of grain.

In 1861, the officers elected were Stephen Clary, President; Clinton Briggs and E. G. Wolcott, First and Second Vice-Presidents. The rebellion had now broken out in this year, and as soon as it was known that Fort Sumpter had been fired upon by the Confederates, the Board commenced its work of equipping and fitting out regiments for the field to sustain the old flag and hold together the Union of the States, firm and imperishable. Nobly did the gallant regiments perform their work, and when their decimated ranks returned home, they brought with them the prestige of having crowned the institution as well as themselves with a halo of glory.

At the election in 1862, C T. Wheeler was elected President; and W. H. Low and John L. Hancock respectively, First and Second Vice-Presidents. The growth of the institution was almost marvelous, both in membership and the value of its transactions. The Board continued to equip and fit out regiments for the field of warfare. It was in this year that General Frank Sherman started for the seat of war, and in doing so passed in review before the members of the Board and was addressed by Ira Y. Munn, Esq. During the summer months, Seth Catlin, Secretary of the Board, died, and John M. Beaty, succeeded to the office.

In 1863, John L. Hancock was elected President, N. K. Fairbank and Charles Randolph, First and Second Vice-Presidents; John M. Beaty and George F. Rumsey, were elected, respectively, Secretary and Treasurer. Mr. Beaty continued in office until 1869 and Mr. Rumsey until 1870. At this time the capacity of the elevators had increased to 8,615,-000 bushels, or an increase of nearly two million bushels in three years.

At the annual election in 1864, Mr. Hancock was re-elected President, and Charles Parker and C. J. Gilbert, Vice-Presidents. This was quite a notable year in the history of the Board; the number of members had reached 1,462, and arrangements were made with the Chamber of Commerce to erect a building on the corner of La Salle and Washington streets, which the Board undertook to occupy for ninety-nine years. The charter of the Board of Trade would only admit of a building and real estate of the value of $200,000, a sum that was thought inadequate to the cost of a lot and a suitable building to meet the demands of its expanded and constantly growing condition. The charter of the Chamber of Commerce did not restrict its power to hold property to any specified amount. Another event of this year was the acceptance of an invitation from the Board of Trade of Boston to visit that city as its guests, with the principal Boards of the country. The high estimation in which the Board of Trade of Chicago was held by the business men of the country at large, was fully demonstrated on this occasion, its entire journey to Boston and return through Canada being a perfect ovation.

At the annual election of April, 1865, Charles Randolph, the present able and popular Secretary of the Board, was elected President, and T. Maple and John C. Dore, First and Second Vice-Presidents. This was a most eventful year. The officials of the Board had but scarcely taken their seats, when the wires spread over the land the sad tidings that Abraham Lincoln, President of the United States, had been assassinated at Washington City. The Board of Trade rooms immediately became the centre of expression of sorrow on that sad event, and the succeeding day after the arrival of the news, a public meeting was held in the Exchange Hall, filling it to repletion. The greatest solemnity and a feeling of deep sadness prevailed among those present. Suitable resolutions were adopted expressive of the public sympathy and sorrow for the great calamity that had fallen upon the country. On the arrival of the remains of the martyred President in this city on May first, the members of the Board turned out *en masse* and took part in the solemn proceedings in conveying to their last resting place the remains of the honored departed, and a large delegation who met the remains on their way hither at Michigan City continued the journey to Springfield.

In May, 1865, the first arrangements were made for the deposit of margins by members of the Board on time contracts. The Confederate armies had now been beaten at all points. General Lee had made his famous surrender at Appomattox Court House to General Grant, and the war had ceased. Then came the disbanding of the volunteer armies of the United States in the field, and on their return home public receptions were given on 'Change to those who had been distinguished as defenders of the Nation, including Generals Grant, Sherman, Webster, Howard and others, and the regiments and battery which had served under the name of the Board of Trade, were given grand receptions, and in each case a splendid banquet by the Board. In June a delegation from the Board, in company with delegations from Milwaukee, St. Louis, and Detroit, visited Boston by invitation of the Boston Board of Trade, which visit accomplished its intention of greatly promoting the business relations between Chicago and Boston. In July the great international convention was held at Detroit, and the Board was largely represented. Its delegates, included such names as the late W. F. Coolbaugh, J. Young Scammon, McChesney, and others equally as prominent, most of whom were conspicuous in the debates and the various discussions that took place in that body. In August, the new Exchange Hall was occupied, and at its opening. the occasion was honored by distinguished visitors from all parts of the country and Canada, and the event was signalized by the most marked, and magnificent series of festivities ever observed in commercial circles in this city. In November, owing to the damp condition of grain then in store

and the continued unfavorable state of the weather, the elevator proprietors advanced the rate of storage to about double the amount charged
previously, in order, as they claimed, to force the grain forward, and into consumption before the close of navigation. This produced great dissatisfaction, and resulted in one of the most exciting and angry meetings
ever held. But the outcome of these proceedings was, that inspectors
appointed by the Board were placed in each of the elevators, whose business it was to keep a knowledge of the receipt and delivery of all grain,
and to report upon its condition when necessary. To the action of the
elevator proprietors on that occasion may be traced all the subsequent
legislative enactments by the State on the subject of grain storage and
inspection. In March, 1866, the Board, with great unanimity, adopted a
memorial to Congress in favor of the passage of a National Bankrupt Law.

In 1866 Hon. John C. Dore was elected President, and P. L. Underwood
and E. W. Densmore, Vice-Presidents. No special incidents of note are
chronicled, but the continued growth and expansive business of the
Board, and its transactions still attracted the attention of the world.

In 1867, Wiley M. Egan was elected President, and Lyman Blair
and C. B. Goodyear, were elected Vice-Presidents. When Mr. Egan
assumed the presidency, the Board was in debt, but when he retired
from the office the indebtedness had been liquidated, and there was
money in the hands of the treasurer.

In 1868, E. V. Robbins was elected President, and E. K. Bruce and
J. D. Cole, Jr., were elected Vice-Presidents. The principal event of
this year was the sending of delegates to Philadelphia for the formation
of a National Board of Trade. The delegates were Wiley M. Egan,
Charles Randolph, Ira Y. Munn and V. A. Turpin.

At the annual meeting in 1869, J. M. Richards was elected President, and Samuel H. McCrea and H. A. Towner, respectively, First and
Second Vice-Presidents. L. V. Parsons was elected Treasurer. To
show the extent to which the business of the Board had reached at this
time, we may mention that the receipts of grain for the year were about
fifty-two and one-half million bushels, to which may be added *over two
million barrels of flour*. In the Spring of this year, John M. Beaty, who
had served most acceptably as Secretary of the Board from the time of
his first election in 1863, tendered his resignation, which was accepted,
and Charles Randolph was elected as his successor, and has, since that
period, filled the official position with marked ability. It is not inappro-
priate at this point to say that Mr. Randolph is now quite a prominent

figure of the Board of Trade. He is a gentleman of large business experience, most decided in the opinions he may entertain, and maintai is them with manly vigor. This characteristic peculiar to him, has, with some people, created a prejudice; but that he is conscientious in his convictions and seeks with an honest purpose to promote the general welfare of the Board, there cannot be a question.

At the annual election in 1870, Samuel H. McCrea was elected President, and B. F. Murphy and W. Dater, respectively, Vice-Presidents, and Charles Randolph, re-elected Secretary. There is nothing of any importance to chronicle during this year.

In 1871, Joseph W. Preston was elected President, and Charles E. Culver and W. N. Brainard, Vice-Presidents, and Orson Smith, Treasurer. During this year there was an extraordinary increase in the receipt of hogs, wool and lumber. The year was made memorable by the occurrence of the great conflagration of the 9th and 10th of October, by which over $150,000,000 worth of property was destroyed, and 120,000 persons rendered homeless. The Board of Trade witnessed the complete destruction of all its records, archives and valuables, as well as of the noble building in which they had been domiciled for over six years, and which had become endeared to them as the scene of many a brilliant triumph in trade. The Chamber of Commerce in addition to a similar experience, lost their building. We need not dwell upon this dark chapter in the history of the Board of Trade. The story of the great conflagration with all of its harrowing details is as familar to our readers as household words.

The Board secured temporary quarters on Canal street immediately after the fire, but the accommodations were meagre and the refuge comfortless. There was a temporary check to the tide of produce that had been setting Chicagoward from all parts of the Northwest. The business prosperity of Chicago for a brief period hung on the balance. The season of navigation would be closed in a few days, and the question was, Can Chicago recover from the terrible shock in time for the transaction of any further business before that event takes place? During that day or two of darkness and doubt, when men wondered whether the city could be or would be rebuilt and rehabilitated, The Board of Trade comprising so much of the wealth, enterprise, energy and courage of the city, had already decided the question. From the cheerless quarters on Canal street, the fiat went forth, "CHICAGO STILL LIVES!" As soon as the vaults of the Board, amid the smouldering debris could be opened and the lease and agreement from the Chamber of Commerce procured therefrom, the following resolution was unanimously adopted:

Resolved, That this Board of Directors hereby notify the Chamber of Commerce corporation, that this Board will comply with the provisions of the lease held from them; and in conformity with that lease, the Board of Trade hereby require that the Chamber of Commerce re-construct at once their building in as good shape as it was originally, and it is the wish of the Board to occupy the building at the earliest possible day.

In response to that resolution, the Chamber of Commerce at once began the work of rebuilding. Two days after the fire, while the ruins were still smoking, men were at work removing the debris. This prompt action of the Board of Trade and Chamber of Commerce had the effect to revive the sinking courage of hundreds of others, and as the determination of those bodies went abroad, by wire and mail, the grand produce wave that had been so lately arrested in its course, flowed on again. A thousand temporary makeshifts were devised, and the wealth of the West commenced again to flow through Chicago. The grain was received and shipped, and the cattle and hogs continued to arrive in greater numbers than before. This crisis was passed, and Chicago, though physically lying in ruins, in spirit was unconquered and unconquerable.

As illustrative of the effect of this action of the Board of Trade, we may mention that in the months of November and December immediately succeeding the fire, the aggregate receipts of grain amounted to 11,863,937 bushels, against 6,818,314 bushels for the corresponding period in 1870, and 6,246,042 bushels in 1869.

The Board, finding their quarters on Canal street entirely too contracted for their purposes, made arrangements for the preparation of a room in the Central Block, on Market street, near Washington, where they continued until the completion of the new Chamber of Commerce building.

In the spring of 1872 J. W. Preston, Esq., was re-elected President, Chas. E. Culver and W. N. Brainard, Vice-Presidents, and Orson Smith, Treasurer. The business of the year showed to extraordinary advantage in comparison with that of previous years. The total shipments for the year were 80,000,000 bushels of grain, against 1,276,593 in 1850. The shipments of corn amounted to over 40,000,000 bushels, against 262,013 bushels in 1859. From the 1st of January, 1872, to October of the same year, the total number of hogs received was 2,136,244, against 757,072 for the whole of the year 1865. During the first nine months of 1872 the number of cattle received was 522,435, an increase of over 90,000 over the number in 1871.

The principal event of the year was the occupation by the Board of the new Chamber of Commerce building on the old site, corner of Washington and La Salle streets, which occurred on the 9th of October, the first anniversary of its destruction. The best skill was employed in its erection, and every detail was watched with the jealous care of architects anxious to make the edifice a monument worthy to secure for them the approbation of all who look upon it. The building was dedicated with appropriate ceremonies on the occasion of its occupation by the Board of Trade—to which allusion has been previously made.

During this year there were periods when general disaster prevailed, arising from the operations of two different firms in their frantic efforts to "corner" the markets, which they succeeded in doing, but each party brought upon themselves the well-merited obloquy of being obliged to "bite the dust." The firm of Chandler, Pomeroy & Co. started in to "corner" the market on oats, and in a short period after a vain attempt to reap a "golden harvest" therefrom, in their visionary idea of an endeavor to buy up all the oats there was in the world (as a witness stated on the stand in open court, such was his belief), they went down with a crash, and for a time their ignoble transactions had clogged the wheels of commerce, and the best and soundest men in the commercial world of Chicago stood para'yzed at the audacious matter that confronted them, and this bankrupt firm finally disappeared from sight. At about this time John B. Lyon buckled on his armor and strode forth the champion of the wheat market, but unfortunately the sheaves that spring from the earth, that glisten and wave in their beauty and play with the sunlight with their treasure, and sleep listlessly in the shadows of night with other collateral matter, were too much for even the over-confident and too zealous Mr. Lyon to handle. His ambitious desires were defeated; his armor became tarnished, and he was laid out a sprawling champion, which sad disaster carried with it a suspension from business of some thirty or forty firms. Here was general consternation, and after Mr. Lyon had gathered himself together he offered 25 per cent. upon his obligations, which was accepted by all his creditors with the exception of two firms—T. H. Seymour & Co. and Dugan, Case & Spear—who, after much litigation in the courts, were paid in full, and Mr. Lyon in

1874 was restored to the privileges of the Board, from which he had been suspended.

The time for holding the annual meeting in the year 1873 had been changed from April to the month of January. At this meeting Charles E. Culver was chosen President. His popularity with the members of the Board was evidenced by the fact that in the balloting there were only two votes cast against him. W. N. Brainard and Howard Priestly were respectively elected First and Second Vice-Presidents. Mr. Randolph and Mr. Smith were re-elected Secretary and Treasurer. At the expiration of Mr. Culver's term in office he was solicited to become a candidate for re-election, but he declined to do so. He was then nominated for a membership on the Committee of Appeals, to which position he was elected by a most decided majority. Without making invidious comparisons it may be truly affirmed that the Board never had a more active, capable and efficient Chief Executive officer than in the person of Mr. Culver. He is a gentleman of slight build, has the unmistakable aspect and air of a man of carefully cultivated mind, refined by the life-long habit of entire conscientiousness, and familiarity with the best society, together with those subtle influences which come of travel, both at home and abroad—he is self poised, rather reticent, wholly modest, entirely self-respecting. No member of the Board has labored with more effectiveness than he, in seeking to purify the commercial character of the Board, and free it from the scandal of corrupt practices. Mr. Culver may be set down as a successful man, thus far in life, and is a living proof of the fact that the completest integrity of Christian principles is no detriment to distinguished success in business. During his incumbency of the office of President of the Board, the financial panic occurred, which proved so disastrous to all our industries; but the Board of Trade proved herself a stanch craft, and weathered the gale without damage. Referring to this most creditable and gratifying fact, President Culver, in his annual report, says: "While many associations similar in character to our own were forced to succumb to the pressure of the panic, and were obliged temporarily to suspend business, this Board of Trade suffered no adjournment of its regular business sessions; and *not one of its members was reported to have failed by reason of the panic.*" In the years 1871, 1872 and 1873 Mr. Culver was the representative of the Board as a delegate to the meetings of the National Board of Trade, which were held in those respective years in the cities of St. Louis, Chicago and Baltimore, and he was honored by that distinguished body by being made one of its Vice-Presidents. Mr. Culver also presided on the memorable occasion of the large and enthusiastic meeting of the members of the Board of Trade, held in the main hall in the year 1872, for the purpose of dedicating the new Chamber of Commerce building to the purposes for which its founders designed it, and which had then been erected and completed on the anniversary day of the great conflagration of the 9th of October 1871.

On the arrival of the delegates in this city in 1873 to attend the meeting of the National Board of Trade, Mr. Culver received the gentlemen representing the various Boards of Trade, and delivered the address of welcome. He also presided on the occasion of the grand banquet at the Grand Pacific Hotel, given in honor of the delegates to the meeting of the National Board of Trade by the members of the Board of Trade of our city, at which were present many prominent and distinguished guests from all parts of the country.

At the annual election held in January, 1874, George M. How was chosen President; Howard Priestly and John R. Bensley, respectively, Vice-Presidents.

Mr. How has been a member of the Board since March, 1855. He was chairman of the Standing Committee in the years 1857 and 1858, under the old organization, and assisted the late Seth Catlin, then Secretary, in compiling the first annual report of the Board of Trade. During the official existence of Julian S. Rumsey, as President, he was earnest and active in assisting that gentleman in instituting reforms, then deemed necessary by the intelligent and active members to keep pace with the growth and increasing business of the Board. At this time the system was inaugurated for grain inspection, which has since been adopted by all the commercial organizations of the country.

In 1868 Mr. How first represented the Board as a delegate to the meetings of the National Board of Trade; and he was subsequently honored in a similar manner by the Board during the years 1869, '72, '73, '75, and 1876. At the meetings of each of the last two years named he was selected by that distinguished body as one of the Vice-Presidents. It was during President How's official term that the "Sturges Corner" came to the surface, and which has since become a matter of public notoriety. Mr. Sturges in his vain desire "to corner" the market came to grief, and involved himself in serious trouble; which has been his companion ever since, on account of irregularities existing, as it was charged, in his business transactions. On October 5th, 1874, complaint was made to the Board of Directors, signed with the names of twenty-four prominent members, setting forth that, "We believe W. N. Sturges is guilty of conduct calculated to degrade our commercial reputation and bring our Association into general disrepute," etc., etc. This complaint was accompanied with specifications, and respectfully and earnestly requested the Board of Directors to investigate the charges, and "in case the charges named, or any of them, are sustained by the evidence that may be submitted that the same may be reported to the Association that it may act upon Mr. Sturges expulsion." The hearing of the complaint was begun before the Board of Directors on the 12th of October, 1874, and was continued until the 6th of November following, which resulted in the following report from the Board of Directors to the Association, to wit: "We have, after mature deliberation, decided that the prosecution have established that Mr. Sturges has been guilty of certain acts which this Board deem and charge to be uncommercial transactions." In the meantime, Sturges served upon the Board of Directors a lengthy document, wherein he refused "to be governed by the rules of the Association, and denied its jurisdiction over him as a member." This document was disregarded by the Board of Directors, for on the 24th of November the balloting for Sturges' expulsion commenced at 10 o'clock A. M., and was continued until 3:35 P. M. An interruption then took place by the service of an injunction procured by Mr. Sturges on an *ex parte* application. At the time of the interruption 937 members had cast their ballots, and 657 of these were for expulsion, while only 279 were against his expulsion. And on the 29th of December, 1874, after the injunction had been dissolved, an opportunity was given to those members of the Board of Trade who had not voted on the previous occasion to cast their ballots, and 39 votes were polled, of which 24 were for expulsion and 15 against expulsion.

On the 27th day of November, 1874, the President and Directors of the Board of Trade filed an answer to the bill which Mr. Sturges had procured upon *ex parte* application. And on the 3d of December a motion to dissolve the injunction was argued before Judge Williams, but the complainant procured a continuance of the same. On the 21st of December the court dissolved the injunction, and on the 28th of December, 1874, the complainant took an appeal to the Supreme Court, and soon after the appeal an order was made by Hon. W. K. McAllister, then one of the justices of the Supreme Court, that the injunction should be continued pending the appeal, and under said injunction the relator continued to exercise the privileges of membership until the 23d of January, 1878, the judgment of affirmance by the Supreme Court of the decree of the Circuit Court dismissing the case not having been entered until January 21, 1878. Mr. Sturges then on the 16th of April made application to the President and the Board of Directors for relief from expulsion, which they declined by a vote of 16 to 1. He then applied for a writ of mandamus before Judge McAllister to compel the Board of Directors to grant him the privileges of a member. This suit was not heard by Judge McAllister, but was removed and heard before Judge Rogers, who tried the case with a jury. Judge Rogers in trying the case gave the jury special instructions that in their conclusion they would simply find for either one of the two parties. The verdict of this jury was favorable to Mr. Sturges, and then the President and Board of Directors appealed this case to the Supreme Court. Mr. Sturges then made an *ex parte* application before Judge McAllister for an injunction to prevent the President and Board of Directors from interfering with his privileges as a member of the Board of Trade pending the appeal. A temporary injunction was granted and the case was then afterwards heard and urged before Judge Farwell, who dissolved the injunction, and Sturges then appealed this case to the Supreme Court and made application before Judge Dickey, of the Supreme Court, to revive the injunction, pending the appeal, which was granted. So that there are now two cases pending in the Supreme Court between W. N. Sturges and the President and the Board of Directors of the Board of Trade.

The foregoing are the principal points in a condensed form of the efforts and the many expedients resorted to by Mr. Sturges to-obtain his re-instatement, with full privileges as a member of the Board of Trade. That he holds the position in high estimation, or that such would greatly accrue to his personal benefit, is evident from the persistent and very determined fight he has made to accomplish his wishes. And it is as equally true of the President and the Directors of the Board of Trade, that they believe Mr. Sturges has in his business transactions trampled upon the dignity and injured the good name of the Board of Trade, from the determined spirit they have manifested in defending their actions in this vexatious matter. In October of this year Alexander Geddes, a member of the Board, who had hitherto been regarded as a gentleman of decided conservative tendencies in his mode of transacting business, ran a successful "corner" in barley. It is seldom that such a result can be recorded, for as a general thing "corners" result in disaster.

At the annual election held in January, 1875, George Armour was elected President; John R. Bensley and D. H. Lincoln, respectively, First and Second Vice-Presidents. The events and experiences of the previous year suggested to the Board of Directors that important modifications should be made in the general rules, and the subject of a revision had been delegated to a committee previous to the date of the last annual meeting, and the result of their labors was duly submitted to the Association and adopted on the 18th of March. This revision did not entirely prove satisfactory and the rules were therefore further revised, and with some important modifications, the revision was re-adopted on the 25th of September, and no further changes took place during this year. Though the code then existing was not considered perfect it was accepted as a compromise. Mr. Armour warmly advocated the maintaining of the lake marine, as the railroads in their management were discriminating in the carrying of freight against the interests of Chicago. And even though the railroads were most of them bankrupt, or fast becoming so, they were formidable competitors against the great free water communication with the East which nature has provided, and says in his annual report: "To our lake marine we must mainly look. The various interests centering in Chicago and other lake cities could better afford to subsidize it than to see it languish and die."

At the annual meeting held in January, 1876, John R. Bensley was elected President; D. H. Lincoln and Josiah Stiles, respectively, First and Second Vice-Presidents. Mr. Randolph and Mr. Smith were re-elected Secretary and Treasurer. During this year there were two decisions rendered by the Supreme Court where four suits against the Board by members who had been subjected to its discipline, were pending, on the appeal of the parties against whom action had been taken. These decisions were in favor of the Board, fully confirming its power to discipline its members under its own rules. The Circuit Court also adjudicated an important question touching the right to demand relief from suspension by a member of the Board, who had been suspended for failure to fulfill commercial contracts, but who had subsequently applied for and obtained a discharge in bankruptcy. The court held that such discharge was not such a satisfactory adjustment and settlement of the obligations of the bankrupt as is contemplated by the rules of the Board. The Board had been much annoyed at former periods by petty suits against members, wherein it was sought to make the Board a party by garnishment of the membership of the member. The Circuit Court held that such membership was not subject to garnishment. The matter of the necessity for some change in the inspection of grain was being pressed upon the attention of the Board, which was placed in the hands of a committee to examine into and report thereon.

At the annual election held in January, 1877, David H. Lincoln was chosen President; Josiah Stiles and William Dickinson First and Second Vice-Presidents. Mr. Lincoln has been a member of the Board for more than 20 years, and during all that period has been an active participant in all matters that tended to perfect or benefit the Association, and at all times commanded the respect and esteem of his business associates. At this time there appears to have been a growing feeling of dissatisfaction among the "members of the Board that the cost of admission to the privileges of membership in the Association, which is deemed desirable to all persons engaged in such branches of business as are usually conducted on 'Change is quite inadequate to the benefits derived by parties who desire to become connected by membership in the Board." This feeling was prompted from the fact that "the organization had grown up from small beginnings to a commanding position in its influence as a commercial body, and a large number of those who by many years' devotion to its advancement may be said to have borne the burden and heat of the day in its early life and maturity. Consequently the old members felt that new-comers should be required to contribute somewhat more adequately for the benefits resulting from a perfected organization, indispensable in the prosecution of the business in which most of the members are engaged." However deeply this feeling may have impressed the membership of the Board, there does not appear in the records that any action had been taken on the matter by the Board of Directors. It seems that there had not been for a year or two any applications for membership on the Board by parties who would make the payment of the regular initiation fee. But those parties who did make application for membership did so with transfers, which had been obtained through the decease of members or from members retiring from the Board, at a much less price than the regular initiating fee, which the rules of the Board permitted. But, however regular this may have been on the part of applicants for membership, the "old-timers" did not take to it kindly.

At the annual meeting held in January, 1878, N. K. Fairbank was chosen President; William Dickinson and John H. Dwight, respectively, First and Second Vice-Presidents. Mr. Randolph and Mr. Smith were respectively elected Secretary **and** Treasurer. This was a very quiet year, nothing of importance having transpired to which we have not already referred. The President of the United States, Rutherford B. Hayes, honored the Board with his presence during the month of **September** and was received by President Fairbank with an address **of** welcome and presented to the members, when he addressed **them** with an agreeable speech of a few minutes **in** recognition of the manner in which he was received. President Fairbank is a gentleman of splendid physique. In this respect, as in all others, he admirably fills the position he holds. He may be numbered among our successful merchants, and worthily wears the respect and esteem **that** is justly due him.

In completing the mention, **as we have now** done, of the **different** administrations of the Board, we deem it proper **to** remark that it **was** our intention at the outset to give a sketch of the important **occurrences** or happenings in each of the successive years intervening **from the inception** of this great commercial body in the year 1848, **to the present time.** Some few of **these** years, as they are herein sketched, are meagre and barren, **in so far as** the relation of events that possibly **may have** occurred incident to **the history of the** Board **of Trade.** If such a deficiency does exist to any material extent, it should be charged to the indifference manifested by those who we thought were the proper parties to obtain such information from, and to whom we made courteous application.

Chicago Board of Trade Transactions.

A FULL EXPLANATION CONCERNING TRADING IN

"FUTURES,"

(COMMONLY CALLED "OPTIONS") AND

SHOWING HOW SETTLEMENTS ARE MADE.

ALSO, AN IMPORTANT U. S. COURT DECISION.

"PUTS AND CALLS."

"FUTURE DELIVERIES."

Among the many matters of importance in which members of the board engage and where the transactions involved are of tremendous magnitude none command more attention—particularly in seasons of largely fluctuating values—than the "trading in contracts for the future delivery" of grain and provisions, more commonly but very improperly called "options." We say improperly, because the contract for the property is fixed and definite, and the only feature in which the trade is at all *optional* is the privilege of delivery *between specified dates*, accorded to the seller or buyer as the trade may be made "seller the month," or "buyer the month." Almost the entirety of trading in "futures," however, is in contracts for "seller the month; the particular month being always specified. Thus, when a dealer "on 'Change" asks of another member the price of "May wheat," each understands the question to apply to the price of contracts for No. 2 Spring wheat, deliverable during the month of May, at the option of the seller as to *what day in May* he will deliver the property. Trades in "buyer the month" are very seldom made and are almost obsolete. The meaning of the phrase "buyer the month" is, however, that the buyer can call for the delivery of the property on any day during May, or any month for which the contract may be made, and the seller is bound to deliver before 2:30 P. M., on the day the demand may be made. On contracts for "seller the month," the contract once made, the seller must deliver the property, and the buyer must receive and pay for it within the time named in the contract, unless the contract shall have been canceled by another offsetting trade, or by "settlement."

To illustrate the detail of a trade in "May wheat," we will suppose that A buys from B 5,000 bushels of wheat, seller May, on 'Change at $1.10 per bushel. In the afternoon A's clerk will present to B a contract, of which the following is the custom accepted and Board of Trade form, which B signs and the contract is complete:

FORM OF CONTRACT.

5,000 Bushels @ $1.10.

GRAIN CONTRACT.   Chicago,...........187

I have this day BOUGHT of *B*.....................

five thousand bushels of No. 2....*Spring Wheat*...............

at one dollar and ten cents per bushel, to be delivered in store, at sel-

ler's option during....*the month of May*, 1878,

To BE DELIVERED IN LOTS OF 5,000 BUSHELS EACH.

This Contract is subject, in all respects, to the Rules and Regulations of the Board of Trade of the City of Chicago.

(Signed)   ....*A*.........................

B signs a similar contract using the word "sold" instead of the word "bought." The above contract calls for No. 2 Spring Wheat. A provision contract is similarly worded, only the kind of property contracted for is named.

By the above contract it will be observed that the seller contracts positively to deliver a specified amount of particularized property. The seller reserving the option as to *time of delivery*, on any day he may elect between the hour of 10 A. M., on May first, until 2:30 P. M., on May 31st, and is the only part of the contract to which the word "option" or its effect in any manner pertains. The property must be absolutely delivered before the expiration of the life of the contract, unless otherwise settled; and in the event of non-delivery after making a demand upon B for its delivery, and B's non-compliance, A can buy the cash property from any one having it to sell, and compel B to pay any difference in amount between such purchase price and the price named in the contract. There is no evading or getting around it on the plea of its being a gambling transaction as is too commonly supposed. The contract is just as valid in justice, equity and law, and as fair as if B had given his contract to A to deliver 100 cords of stone or 100,000 bricks to be delivered within the time specified on the wheat contract, and B is just as absolutely liable to A for damages resulting from the non-fulfilment of his grain or provision contract as he would be if he failed to deliver the stone or the brick. In a failure on B's part to deliver the stone or brick, in accordance with his contract, both common custom and law would justify A in buying either of these articles at the market price as soon as said contract had expired unfulfilled, and A could by law collect from B any difference in the price he may have to pay, beyond the named price in the contract; and the courts have of late established by several decisions the absolute legality of time contracts for the future delivery of grain and provisions made under Chicago "Board of Trade" rules, as evidenced by the following decision by the Supreme Court of Illinois at the September term of 1875 in the case of Woolcott et al. vs. Heath (Ill. Reports, vol. 78, page 437). The Court's decision was as follows:

＊ ＊ "Time contracts, made in good faith, for the future delivery of grain or any other commodity, are not prohibited by the common law, nor any statute of this State, nor by any policy beneficial to the public welfare. Such a restraint would limit commercial transactions to such a degree as could not but be prejudicial to the best interests of trade. Our present statute was not in force when these dealings were had; consequently the rights of the parties are not affected by it. What the law, prohibits, and what is deemed detrimental to the public interests, is speculation in differences in market values, called, perhaps, in the peculiar language of the dealers 'puts' and 'calls,' which simply means a privilege to deliver or receive the grain, or not, at the seller's or buyer's option. It is against such ficticious, gambling transactions, we apprehend, the penalties of the law are leveled."

Again, in the case of Pixley et al. vs. Boynton et al., (79th Ill. Reports, page 353) the Court rendered this opinion (September term, 1875):

＊ ＊ "Seller the month, as that term is understood and used on the Board of Trade, is explained to mean the seller has until the last day of the month in which to make a delivery of any grain contracted to be sold. Under such a contract, as we understand the evidence, all the option the seller has is the privilege to deliver the grain at any time before the maturity of the contract. This is nothing more than a time contract, which is regarded on the Board of Trade and elsewhere as a legitimate and regular contract. Time contracts in relation to grain as well as other commodities, are of daily occurence, and must necessarily be in commercial transactions. * * * The intention of the parties (page 354) gives character to the transaction; and if either party contracted in good faith he is entitled to the benefit of his contract, no matter what may have been the secret purpose or intentions of the other party."

The Supreme Court has never yet decided against the validity or legality of time contracts, and it will be seen by the following ruling that the idea apparently so long prevalent among home as well as outside dealers that contracts for the purchase and sale for future delivery were held illegal by the Supreme Court of Illinois, was erroneous. The summary of the decision of the Supreme Court, recently rendered, in the case of Musick & Brown *vs.* B. F. Logan was as follows:

* * "It is clear that the parties were not dealing in options, but that the plaintiffs were instructed to buy for the defendant a certain amount of grain for future delivery, and actually bought it. Under the contract made Logan did not have the *option* to buy, but he actually purchased, and if he failed to take the grain at the time he was to receive it he would be bound to respond in damages. So with the parties of whom the grain was bought. They did not have an *option* to sell, *but actually sold the grain,* and were bound to deliver it at the time specified, or. on failure, would be liable to damages. The statute does not prohibit a party from selling or buying grain for future delivery; such was not the purpose of the statutes; nor can it make any difference as to the legality of the contract whether the party who sells for future delivery, at the time the sale was made, has on hand the grain; a party may sell to-day a certain quantity of grain for delivery in a week or a month hence, and then go upon the market and buy the grain to fill the contract. It is true the defendant *had the option to select a day within a limited time on which he would receive the grain,* but such an option does not fall within the statutes, for the reason that it does not render the sale optional. We are, therefore satisfied that the contracts did not fall within the statute, and we perceive no reason why they should not be enforced. The judgment of Circuit Court will be affirmed."

The italics are our own.

These decisions render collectable by law any indebtedness arising from dealing in contracts for the future delivery of grain or provisions, other opinions to the contrary, notwithstanding. Dealing in futures is, on the part of commission merchants, a business of unusual risk. unless said commission houses adhere strictly and inexorably to the idea of "full cash margins absolutely in hand" before trades are begun. Many well meaning and honorably disposed commission men have been utterly ruined by accepting and executing orders and drawing *time* bills upon their customers for the required margins, and, in many instances, sight drafts have been returned dishonored, where the violent fluctuations of the market have gone largely against the party ordering, even before a sight draft could reach the party ordering the deal made, and to whom it would be plain that whatever he might pay would be dead loss. In times of large fluctuations the market value of grain may vary 6c, 8c, 10c, 12c, 15c, and even 20c in a single day. We will illustrate a case in point. Mr. Smith, of Charleston, S. C., may order M & W to buy for him 20,000 bushels wheat seller May, and authorize M & W to draw on him for the customary 10c a bushel, or $2,000 margin. M & W may execute the order, say at $1.20, and make sight draft for the amount of the margin, say $2,000. Foreign or other news may come next day and very unfavorably affect the market as regards Mr. Smith's interests, and a decline of 4c or 5c be established on the succeeding day, the markets may still be more unfavorably affected, and prices again decline 3c, 4c, or 5c, making, say a total decline of 8c to 10c on the third day. M & W's drafts would reach Charleston and be presented to Mr. Smith, who could ill afford to lose the $2,000, and he being advised of the decline by the daily papers or dispatches from M & W would say to himself, "If I pay the drafts I pay out all the ready money I have, and will, of course, know that the amount I might pay would be all exhausted by the decline of the last two days, and besides, if I do pay, M & W will at once want $2,000 *additional* margin, which it is quite impossible for me to put up. I guess I won't pay, and maybe by the time the draft gets back the market may rally, in which event I can order them to redraw," but the market don't rally. M & W's banker advise them that Mr. Smith don't pay his draft, and that they must pay $2,000 to the bank at once, to make the amount credited to them for the draft good. M & W will then be either compelled to sell the wheat out at a loss and take their chances of collecting the balance from Mr. Smith (which chance would, of course, be very remote), and not being disposed to put up $2,000 more margin on a deal which they have made for Mr. Smith, they reluctantly close the trade by sale, pocket a $2,000 loss, make up Mr. Smith's account, send it to him, request immediate remittance, etc. Mr. Smith replies: "Sorry, but couldn't help it; ordered the wheat for a friend who positively promised to have the money ready when the draft for margins should be presented; the friend had cruelly disappointed him; would do what he could to collect; hoped that he might soon have a little money he could send them on a trade as margin in which he could make back the loss for them, and would see that they never lost a cent," etc., etc. Weeks, and perhaps months, would roll round. M & W would notify Mr. S. that he must settle or they would collect by suit. Mr. Smith would answer this time (not so sorry), and would say "sue and be d—d; it's a gambling debt, and you can't collect a cent." Not very honorable in Mr. Smith, of course, but that is Mr. Smith's way, and so the matter would rest. During the year M & W might make a dozen such losses, and wind up at the end of the year with the $20,000 capital originally invested in their business, exhausted in paying margins for other people, and finally be forced to stop business because there means were exhausted This is simply the history of hundreds of houses who have started and failed in the option trade in Chicago.

"PUTS AND CALLS."

What are commonly known as "Puts" and "Calls" on the Board of Trade are the pet antipathy of the legitimate dealer, and are regarded with chronic aversion by all conservative traders. They are not recognized as legal by the Statutes of the State, and "differences" resulting from trades based thereon are not collectable under Board of Trade rules. Within the past year they have been exorcised from the "Rooms" of the "Board" and trading in them by members, in the "Main Hall" or during regular 'Change hours is forbidden under penalty of fine or expulsion; and yet, however illegal or irregular they may be, the volume of trading done in them after the regular session of the Board, amounts to hundreds of thousands of bushels daily, and compassing as many hun-

dreds of thousands of dollars in value. There being no legal responsibility, they are made entirely "on honor," as no member of the Board
can enter complaint against another member to the directory for default-
ing upon a "privilege," *i. e.* a "put" or "call," nor upon any deal based
upon a "privilege." To many of our readers these terms are **mean-
ingless** without further explanation, and it will now be our province to
attempt, at least, to make clear the detail incident to privilege trading.
A "put" means that the **seller thereof** sells to the buyer thereof **the**
privilege of having delivered to himself (the seller) **by the** buyer **5,000**
bushels of any named grain, at any stated price, and for any stated time
of delivery. To make this more clear we will illustrate by supposing
that A sells to B a "put," that is, A sells to B the privilege **of putting or**
delivering to him (A) 5,000 bushels of May wheat on the succeeding day
for $10, at $1.09 per bushel. If the price did not go below $1.09 **the**
next day, B would not **"put" the wheat** as there would be no profit in so
doing, but **he (B) would lose the** $10 he paid A for **the** "put." If, how-
ever, the market should decline to $1.07 the next day, B could then buy
5,000 bushels May wheat of C or any other party at $1.07 and deliver it
to A on his "put" at **$1.09 and** would therefore secure a profit of 2c. per
bushel or **$100, making** a clear gain of $90, $10 having been paid for the
"put." The life of a "put" extends only until the close of 'Change hours
on the **day succeeding the one on** which the purchase of **the** privilege **or**
"put" is made, unless a more extended time is agreed upon between the
contracting parties. A "call" **is quite similar in results. We will sup-**
pose that to-day A sells to B a "call" on May wheat for **to-morrow for
the** usual $10 at say $1.10½. The morrow comes and **wheat advances to
$1.12. At any** time during the day B can sell 5,000 bushels of wheat **at
$1.12 and "call" A to** deliver at the $1.10½ the agreed "call" **price.** The
moment B "calls" the wheat he becomes the buyer of it at the "call"
price, and if he can sell it at $1.12 he **can secure a** profit of 1½c. per
bushel or $75 less the $10 he has paid for the **"call."** The "put" or "call"
is secured simply by the buyer **notifying the seller verbally or by** proxy
any time before the bell strikes the 3:30 P. M. hour.

The difference between a "put" or a "call" and a regular **trade in**
"futures" is simply this: In buying for "future delivery" an absolute contract is made to deliver or secure a certain amount of specified property
at a stipulated price. If, however, you buy a "put" or "call" you simply
buy the *privilege* of delivering or receiving the property. It being entirely optional with the purchaser of the "privilege" whether he makes a

positive trade or not, and while it is clearly a misnomer to apply the word "option" to a *contract* for future delivery, it is quite as clearly the proper title to apply to a trade in a "privilege," *i. e.* a "put" or a "call." These privileges are largely dealt in by operators in "futures," who use them as "insurance" on their legitimate trades, *i. e.* protection against loss beyond the figure named on the "put" or "call" trade. This we will illustrate by supposing that A having bought 50,000 bushels of wheat during the day at say $1.10 for "May," and being a little nervous about his margin drafts not being paid, or, if on his own account, desires to lose not over 1c. per bushel in the event of the decline, he would insure himself against more than the 1c. per bushel loss by buying *after* regular 'Change hours a "put" on 50,000 bushels May wheat from B, C and D, at $1.09; he could then, in the event of a decline below $1.09, deliver the wheat on the "puts" he has on B, C and D, and thus prevent loss beyond that amount plus the amount he may have paid for the "puts;" and on the other hand, if A should be short 50,000 bushels of wheat at $1.10, he could protect himself from a loss of more than 1c. a bushel by purchasing from B, C and D 50,000 bushels of "calls" on May wheat at say $1.11 for next day, and in the event of the market advancing to $1.12, or over, he would be "insured" against more than 1c. per bushel loss by "calling" on B, C and D to deliver to him the 50,000 bushels on the "calls" bought of them, which he could in turn deliver to the parties he might sell to at $1.12 or over. The following ruling indicates the position of our courts in regard to the legality of "puts" and "calls," or "privileges:"

In the case of Pickering *et. al. vs.* Chase (79th Ill. Reports, page 328) the Court decided: "A contract for the sale and future delivery of grain, by which the seller has the privilege of delivering or not delivering, and the buyer the privilege of calling or not calling for the grain, just as they choose, and which on its maturity is to be filled by adjusting of differences in market value, is but an optional contract in the most objectionable sense, and, being in the nature of a gambling transaction, the law will not tolerate it."

From the above it will be seen that the Supreme Court has never decided against the validity of option contracts. The decisions (as per last quoted) have been against "puts" and "calls," and the Chicago Board of Trade, like the Supreme Court, disclaims these latter as illegitimate transactions. Thus it will be seen that the idea, apparently so long prevalent among home as well as outside dealers, that *all* contracts for the purchase and sale for future delivery were held illegal by the Supreme

Court of Illinois, was erroneous—the Court merely said that "puts" and
"calls" are gambling operations.

The usual difference in price on "puts" and "calls," on what on a
steady market is usually from ½ to 1c. per bushel from the *closing* price
on the Board.   Thus if "May wheat" closes at $1.10, the price of "calls"
on an ordinary quiet market would be from $1.10½ to $1.11, and the
price of "puts" from $1.09½ to $1.09.   In seasons of violent fluctuations,
however, a wider range of prices obtains, and the "put" or "call" value
will be 1, 2, 3 or even 5c. per bushel above or below the closing prices
on 'Change.   Our illustrations are based upon the average ruling differences on a steady market.

These privileges are often bought and sold for much longer terms
than the succeeding day, and occasionally extend fifteen, thirty and even
sixty days.   The prices at which these *extended* privileges are made,
vary largely, and in proportion to the time compassed, a "call" for buyer
"the month" usually commands a premium of 5 to 10c. per bushel from
the ruling value on the day the "call" is sold, and about the same difference on a "put" for the same period.

"OPTION TRADING."

SETTLEMENTS AND MARGINS.

To parties who are not familiar with the "deal," one of the most
puzzling features incident to trading in options (*i e.* contracts for future
delivery) is the *modus operandi* of making settlements or "ringing the
deals" as it is more commonly designated.   Strangers visiting the Board
of Trade will notice around and near a long upright desk, at the north-
east end and side of the room, around and near which during 'Change
hours, quite a crowd of lads and some adults congregate, and who are
constantly calling out the names of the different firms who trade in
"options," and who are constantly comparing entries in small memorandum books which they carry, with each other, and who will be heard
remarking as they conclude their calculations: "You pay A $175 and

collect $37.50 from C," or "All right, we pay $62.50," etc. etc., which is all Greek to the looker on and understandable only by those who are engaged in the option trade. We will endeavor to make plain, as briefly as possible, how settlements are made: First of all it must be undertsood that the trading in option deals in grains and provisions is always for lots of 5,000 bushels each, and in pork and lard for 250 packages of either; any amount other than these are *irregular* trades and seldom made, and when made can never be settled unless settled direct.

It is easy enough to understand that if A buys 5,000 bushels of May wheat from B to-day at $1.06 and sells it to B to-morrow or next week at $1.07 that B will owe A 1 cent a bushel or $50, and that the two trans-actions settle each other's books, so far as this trade is concerned. But suppose A buys 5,000 bushels of May wheat (*i. e.*, wheat deliverable at *seller's option* any time during May) from B to-day at $1.06; then let it be supposed that A wishes to close his trade to-morrow, but that B wishes to let his deal stand—don't want to sell. Then A must sell to some other party, which he does, and sells 5,000 May wheat to C at $1.08. This sale made, A's books will be even, *so far as the amount of wheat is concerned*, that is, he will have 5,000 bought and 5,000 bushels sold, but he will have two deals open, 5,000 bought of B and 5,000 sold to C. The next move to be made is to "settle" or "ring" the deals, and clear them from the books. This may be done when B buys 5,000 bushels wheat from C, or from any party who may have sold it to A. Let us suppose that a few days thereafter B does buy from C 5,000 bushels of May wheat at $1.08½; as soon as these trades are made they are reported to the settling clerks, who are continually comparing purchases and sales, and it is found that B has bought the 5,000 bushels from C; a ring is at once made, and it will stand as follows on the settlement books of each, viz:

A bought of B 5,000 bu. May wheat at $1.06. B bought of C 5,000 bu. May wheat at $1.08. C bought of A 5,000 bu. May wheat at $1.08½. A collected $100 from B and $25 from C. B collects $25 from C. By the above it will be seen that A has made $125 profit, and that C loses $25 and B loses $100, and the trades are entirely cleared from the books of each party, whereas each party had 5,000 bu. bought and 5,000 bu. sold on their respective books until the "ring" or settlement was made. These settlements often compass five, seven, ten, and sometimes, though seldom, twelve or fifteen different firms before the ring is complete. We will give one more illustration of a larger "ring," comprising say seven different parties, and which we will suppose to be in corn, viz: A buys

5,000 bu. April corn at 42c. of B. B buys 5,000 bu. of C at 41½c. C
buys 5,000 bu. of same option of D at 43c. D buys same amount of E
at 44c. E buys 5,000 of F at 44½c, and F may in a day or two buy 5,000
of A at 44c. The settlement clerks in the half-hourly comparisons would
readily discover the ring and proceed to close the trades up. The memorandum on the settlement books would show as follows:

A bought of B 5,000 bu. April corn at 42c.

B bought of C 5,000 bu. April corn at 41½c; B's gain, $25.

C bought of D 5,000 bu. April corn at 43c; C's loss, $75.

D bought of E 5,000 bu. April corn at 44c; D's loss, $50.

E bought of F 5,000 bu. April corn at 44½c; E's loss, $25.

F bought of A 5,000 bu. April corn at 44c; F's gain, $25.

A having bought at 42c and sold at 44c, gains $100.

In the above transactions the party making the largest profit would,
as a rule, collect from all loosers in the "ring" and pay those who have a
profit besides themselves. In the above A would collect $75 from C, $50
from D, and $25 from E, making a total of $150, and would pay B $25
and F $25, leaving the $100 gained in hand, and the books of all the
parties interested would be cleared of the trades named.

All members of the board are expected to pay the balances they
may owe the day the settlement is made, or at farthest on the next day.
The failure on the part of any member of the Board to pay balances
due on settlements on demand renders such member liable to suspension
from the privileges of the Board immediately upon the complaint of the
party unpaid.

One of the most unpleasant positions that option traders find themselves in occasionally, is to have large deals out with "one-sided" operators—those whose trades may be entirely on either the bull or the bear
side. To show how awkwardly unpleasant such a situation may be made
to a trader in options who happens to get long to a one-sided "short"
and short to a one-sided "long," operator, we will suppose that A, a
commission merchant, one who does a *strictly commission* business in
"futures," receives to-day an order from John Jones, of Jonesville, to
buy for his account 100,000 bu. of May wheat at the market value, and
remits to A $10,000 margin. A at once goes into the market and may buy
to the extent of 40,000 bu. of May wheat of Y, a strong believer in
lower prices, at $1.06, and 60,000 bu. of same option of H, another large
dealer and prominent operator, also on the bear side, at $1.06¼. In the
course of a day or two Mr. Jones, of Jonesville, by an advance in prices,

being able to realize a profit of 2c per bu. orders A to "sell his wheat." Upon receipt of Mr. J's order A at once offers and sells at say $1 08 50,000 bu. to Mr. A heavy dealer on the bull side, and 50,000 bu. to F, another heavy bull operator, at $1.08¼. This being done, A makes up Mr. Jones' account, remits him his $10,000 margin, and the $2,000 profit, less his (A's) commission of $250. This lets Mr. Jones out of the deal, *but A has 200,000 bu. of unsettled wheat deals on his books.* The bears, Y and H, of whom he bought the wheat, still believing that lower prices must prevail, decline to buy any wheat, and M and F continuing firm in *their* convictions, refuse to sell a bushel. A, therefore, is unable to settle a bushel of either his "bought" or his "sold" wheat. A decline of 4c or 5c may now occur, and Y and H finding the deal going in their favor, and against A, call on him to deposit 10c a bu. margin, or $10,000. This $10,000 must be put up within one hour after the call is made, according to the established rules of the Board, and is promptly deposited by A, who can in turn call Y and H and force them to deposit a similar amount. The decline, however, makes A's sale to M and F against them and in his favor, and he accordingly, as a prudent man, calls on them to deposit 10c a bu. margin, or $10,000, which they do, and as is their right, call back upon A to put up a like amount, which he is necessitated to do within the specified hour. This makes a total of $20,000 margin A has been forced to deposit on the trades he has made for Mr. Jones, of Jonesville, and Mr. Jones' margins and profits have been paid him, and so far as Mr. Jones is concerned the trade closed, while A has some 200,000 bushels of wheat on his books that can't be settled, and his $20,000 margin must remain up, until it can be settled by Y and H buying May wheat or M and F selling. In the event. of neither of these parties changing their opinions, and continuing to stand on their trades, A will have to wait until the maturity of the May option contract comes round, when Y and H will be compelled to deliver him the cash wheat he has bought from them, "seller May," and which he can in turn deliver to M and F, and thus close the deal with both parties by the delivery of the cash wheat. Margins must be put up within one hour after being called, if the call is made before 2 o'clock P. M.; if made after 2 P. M., it must be up by 11 A. M. next day. The failure to respond to a call for margin is generally considered a failure in fact, and so acted upon by the parties interested. The rule relating to margins we here annex. It reads as follows:

RULE XXIII.

MARGINS ON TIME CONTRACTS.

SECTION 1. On time contracts purchasers shall have the right to require of sellers, as security, ten (10) per cent. margins based upon the contract price of the property bought, and further security, from time to time, to the extent of any advance in the market value above said prices. Sellers shall have the right to require as security from buyers ten (10) per cent. margins on the contract price of the property sold, and in addition any differences that may exist or occur between the estimated legitimate value of any such property and the price of sale. All securities or margins shall be deposited either with the Treasurer of the Association or with some bank duly authorized by the Board of Directors to receive such deposits; *provided*, such deposit shall not be made with any bank or banks to which the party calling for the said security or margin shall expressly object at the time of making such a call.

The first of the month (Sundays excepted) is usually quite an exciting day in the vicinity of the Board of Trade building, in consequence of the large deliveries of grain and provisions that are generally made on that day. To illustrate: A having sold B 5,000 bushels March wheat, he (B) can, on the first of March, or any day during the month, deliver it, and those dealers who have received cash property during February generally deliver on March 1 on such "sold" contracts as they may have out "seller March," unless they are on the bull side at the time, in which event they would prefer to carry it, so as not to affect the market unfavorably, by letting the property out. One 5,000 bushel lot of wheat may be made to fill a dozen sales within an hour after it is put out. The deliveries must be made by or before 2:30 P. M.; if such delivery is not made before 2:30 P. M. the purchaser can refuse to receive the grain, pork, or lard, as the case may be, until next day. As a consequence, on the first of the month, between 2 P. M. and 2:30 P. M. there is unusual excitement in the vicinity named, caused by the delivery clerks flying along the streets with the bills and warehouse receipts to complete these deliveries before the 2:30 P. M. bell may strike. Their progress is often much impeded by the crowd standing on the sidewalks to see the fun, and personal collisions are not infrequent, and when they occur are generally severe and occasionally serious. The moment the bell strikes the

2:30 hour no more tenders can be made, and the delivery clerks are often "stuck," much to their chagrin, by being but one-quarter of a minute too late, and the discomfited youth retires somewhat chop-fallen amid the jeers of the crowd, which heartily applauds those who are just in time to be successful in completing the delivery, and who quite as heartily "cod" with groans and hand-clapping the unfortunate wight who is just in time to be "out of time."

The following is the form of certificate issued by the banks receiving margin deposits:

CHICAGO,.............................18 .

.....................................has deposited with this Bank ....Dollars, as margin or security on a contract or contracts between the depositor and....................... which amount is payable on the return of this certificate or its duplicate duly endorsed by both of the above-named parties, or on the order of the President of the Board of Trade of the city of Chicago, indorsed on either the original or duplicate hereof, as provided by the rules of said Board of Trade, under which the above-named deposit has been made.

..............., Cashier.

A FEW REMARKS CONCERNING OPTION TRADING.

Trading in "options" or contracts for the delivery of grain or provisions at periods subsequent to the date of the contract, at the option of the seller or buyer, is a business to which a considerable number of the heaviest and most responsible firms on the Board of Trade devote almost their entire attention. The word "option" is, strictly speaking, a misnomer. However, as the word (incorrect as it may be) is most commonly used among dealers in "futures," we will accept the custom and use the word "option" in our explanations which we herein propose to give. The value of business transacted in active seasons, in this line, is simply enormous, the dealings of single firms amounting to a million or more dollars in value in a single day.

Of the nineteen hundred members of the Chicago Board of Trade it is safe to assert that at least three-fourths of the entire membership operate either for themselves or on commission for others. Owing to the violent fluctuations of the market at times, the business is attended with more than the usual amount of the risk, and the greatest amount of care is essential on the part of commission merchants trading for country parties, in the closing of deals before the expiration of the customary margins consequent upon the fluctuations of the market, which rarely remains at the same figure a quarter of an hour at a time for a whole week, and during the week often fluctuates several cents per bushel on grain, and fifty cents to one dollar a barrel on mess pork.

In moments of these violent changes in values, the excitement is almost indescribable, and the frantic buyers and sellers, to an outsider at such times, have more the appearance of so many hundred lunatics, rather than the quickest thinking business men of the country.

A very large amount of business is done in this market in "option trading" we herewith give an explanation of such business transactions:

"Option Deals" are the result of a desire on the part of operators and dealers to buy grain or provisions for a rise, or sell for a decline, in the future, and the regular rule is to buy or sell, "seller the month," or any future month.

The following are the terms used and an explanation of their meaning as generally understood by the trade

A "Buyer's Option" gives the buyer the right to demand from the seller the delivery of the property bought, any day during the time specified in the contract, and when not demanded the seller can and must deliver before 2:30 o'clock of the last day of the life of the option.

A "Seller's Option" gives the seller the right to deliver the property sold, any day during the time specified in the contract, and he must deliver it before 2:30 o'clock P. M. of the last day of the life of the option.

To secure the faithful carrying out of these contracts, margins not exceeding 10 per cent. upon the value of the property specified in the contract, may be demanded by both buyer and seller at the time the trade is made, or subsequently; and thereafter during the continuance of the contract the seller may require the buyer to keep good 10 per cent. margin below the shipping value of the property, and the buyer may require the seller to keep good 10 per cent. margin above the current value in this market.

Margins must be deposited in a bank which has filed sufficient bonds with the Board of Trade, within one banking hour after they are called, (provided the call is made before 11 A. M., and if made at or after 11 A. M. the party called upon has until 2 P. M., the time between 11 A. M. and 1 o'clock P. M., being the regular change hours, is exempted from the rule of one hour as above) the bank giving its receipt for the amount so deposited, payable to the order of the buyer and seller jointly, which receipt requires the indorsement of both parties to the contract upon being surrendered.

Contracts are made to cover any length of time ahead; but, without waiting the maturity of a contract, it can be closed by the commission merchant making a purchase if "short," or a sale if "long," and thus a trade can be closed, at the dealer's option, any time between the date and maturity of the contract. But little capital (margins only) is required, and no expense, save commissions, attach to option trades. The requisite margin generally required by the commission merchant, and expected by him to be kept good in case of adverse change in the market, is 10 per cent. of the market valuation, or such an amount as may be agreed upon between the commission merchant and his customer. The commission merchant, however, is at all times liable to be called the full 10 per cent. of the face value of the contract, and can be compelled to put up that amount on one hour's notice, and also such further amount as the fluctuations of the market may increase that liability.

All grain is sold during summer storage (from April 15 to November 15) subject to 1¼ cents, and during winter storage subject to 4 cents per bushel storage, and the receipts on delivery must have five days to run.

Winter storage commences November 15 and ends April 15. All grain except "Rejected" and "No Grade," in store or received between these dates, after 4 cents storage has accrued on it will be subject to no further charges until after April 15.

As the parties who finally take the grain out of store, pay the full storage to the elevators, dealers can, therefore, hold grain here all through winter storage, or any length of time between November 15 and April 15, free of storage, if they sell in this market.

The commissions on option deals, which include both buying and selling, are one-quarter cent. per bushel on grain in 5,000 bushel lots; and one-half per cent. on provisions in lots of not less than $2,000 in value.

No further expense is incurred, unless the commission merchant is required to pay for and carry the property, in which case it turns into a cash deal, in which event an extra commission is usually charged.

To commission men we would remark right here, by way of warning, a suggestion or two, which, if carefully regarded, will prevent trouble.

The risks attending this line of business are much greater than in handling cash property, and it behooves all careful, prudent men that they look to it closely, that all option trading be initiated and closed upon the safest conservative business basis.

In all cases, *without exception*, require your margins absolutely in hand before opening a trade. In filling orders for parties residing out of the city, require of them at the time when they forward an order to buy or sell, to deposit, with a responsible bank, the required margin subject to your order; and instruct the cashier thereof to notify you of the receipt of such deposit by telegraph, and in no case open a trade until such notification be received. If parties order a trade made and say they will remit by mail, be sure that the parties are men of their word and will do as they agree. Do not be so anxious to do business as to accept margins that are too small. The folly of attempting to operate on attenuated or too meagre margins is too obvious to be discussed. The majority of the failures that occur on the Board of Trade can be mainly traced to the fact that too much trading has been done on *too small margins*. Make it your duty for your own protection, as well as for the protection of your reliable customers, to discourage "over-trading" by always requiring full and ample margins from all.

EXPENSES.

Expenses attending the buying and shipping of grain. Storage, which must be paid by the shipper upon all kinds of grain, when drawn from store—between the 15th of April and 15th of November—is 1¼c per bushel, and during the balance of the year—say from the 15th of November to the 15th of April—4c per bushel. Upon all grain shipped by lake, the charges, other than for storage as above, are fire insurance (during the time of loading), say 2 days at 10c per $100; marine insurance varying according to time of year, from ¼ per cent. to 3 per cent. Inspection aboard—say 25c per 1,000 bushels, and commissions—and upon all grain shipped by railroad from store, the charges, other than for storage, are, for fire insurance same as upon lake shipments; for switching cars to elevator $2 per car; for trimming cars $1 per car; for inspection aboard 25c per car, and for commissions. On all grain brought "by sample" "free on board" there are ordinarily no charges save commissions.

Cost of buying and carrying grain in store. Charges accruing upon grain in store are: For storage ½ cent per bushel for each 10 days or part thereof; fire insurance at an average for the different elevators, say 2½ to 3 per cent. per annum, interest at 10 per annum, and commissions. This during the term of summer storage, say from the 15th April to the 15th November; and from the last named date, storage accumulates as above stated, up to 4c per bushel, when no more accrues until the 15th of April, when summer storage again obtains. Other charges for carrying are the same at all times during the year.

U. S. DISTRICT COURT, W. D. WISCONSIN.

CHARLES EDWARD CLARK Assignee of C. B. STEVENS et al. v. SYLVESTER D. FOSS et al.

BOARD OF TRADE CONTRACTS—CONTRACT TO DELIVER AT A FUTURE DAY—OPTION CONTRACTS.

BUNN, J.—This is a suit in equity begun by the assignee of C. B. Stevens & Sons, bankrupts, to set aside and cancel six certain promissory notes for the sum of $1,231.10 each, aggregating $7,386.60, and a mortgage upon real estate at De Soto, in Vernon county, Wis., to secure the same, executed by C. B. Stevens & Sons, to the defendants, Dec. 1, 1874, on the ground that the same are void as being given to secure a consideration arising out of certain option contracts for the sale and delivery of grain, which it is claimed were wagering contracts, under the laws of Illinois in force at that time.

The bankrupts were, and for many years prior to the fall of 1874, when these transactions occurred, had been merchants and dealers in grain and produce upon the Mississippi river at DeSoto, Wis., and as such had for several years purchased and shipped wheat and other grain to the defendants, who were commission merchants at Chicago, and members of the Board of Trade, for twenty years or more, doing business under the firm name of S. D. Foss & Co., and had, also, from time to time, specu- lated in grain in the Milwaukee market, and also in the Chicago market, through the defendants, acting as their factors and commission merchants at that place. They were then in good financial circumstances, though with small capital; had a running account, and were in good credit and stand- ing with S. D. Foss & Co. In October, 1874, the bankrupts ordered de- fendants at different times, by telegraph, to make sales of grain for them upon the Chicago market for November delivery, amounting in the ag- gregate to 70,000 bushels of corn, and 5,000 or 10,000 bushels of wheat. The defendants, upon receiving these orders, went upon the market in Chicago and executed them by making, as was the custom, contracts gen- erally in writing, and in their own name, with different parties for the sale of the grain for November delivery, in lots of 5,000, or multiples of 5,000 bushels; and immediately and from time to time notified bankrupts by telegram and by letter of what they had done, and their acts were fully ratified and approved by the bankrupts. No "margins" were re- quired to be put up by C. B. Stevens & Co., as they had an account with defendants, and were accounted by them responsible.

At about the time or a little before these contracts matured, as they did on the last day of November, the defendants performed a part of them on the behalf of C. B. Stevens & Sons, by a purchase and actual de- livery of the grain to the parties to whom the sales were made. The evidence shows that as to 20,000 bushels of corn there was an actual de- livery of the grain, and as to 10,000 more a delivery of warehouse re- ceipts for that amount. As to the balance of the grain contracted to be sold, the defendants went upon the market and purchased it of different parties and had it ready for delivery; and then finding other parties who had similar deals for November purchases and sales, formed rings or tem- porary clearing houses through which by means of a system of mutual offsets and cancellations that had grown upon the board, the contracts were settled by an adjustment of differences, saving an actual delivery and change of possession. It so happened that there was a considerable rise in the market price of corn during the month of November; and it was found that after these transactions were closed out there had been a loss to C. B. Stevens & Sons, of something over $10,000, and which the defendants having paid in cash for them on the purchase of the grain debited to their account according to the previous course of dealing between the parties.

The notes and mortgage in suit were soon afterward given by the bankrupts to secure a portion of these sums so advanced by the defendants for them, including also about $375 charged by S. D. Foss & Co. as their commissions. Unsecured notes were also given for $3,000 balance of the $10,386.60 indebtedness, which were afterwards paid by C. B. Stevens & Sons.

Two years afterwards, on Nov. 19, 1876, C. B. Stevens & Sons, filed their petition in bankruptcy in this court, and were on the same day adjudged bankrupts. The assignee in bankruptcy brings this suit to set aside the notes and mortgage, and in substance claims that C. B. Stevens & Sons at the time the orders for the sale of grain were made and executed in October, 1874, had no corn to sell and no expectation of having any with which to fill these contracts. That these facts were known to both parties that is, to the bankrupts, and to the defendants S. D. Foss & Co., and that it was understood by and between them at the time that no grain was in fact to be delivered by C. B. Stevens & Sons, but that the contracts were to be settled by the payment or receipts of differences, according as the market should rise or fall in the month of November, and that they were thus mere wagers upon the November market, and as such, contrary to law and void, and that the notes and mortgage confessedly given to secure cash advances made by defendants as the factors of the bankrupts, and with their approval, to pay the losses sustained upon these sales should be canceled and delivered up.

The question is whether this should be done.

This question is, of course, a mixed question of fact and law. But I regard it as more a question of fact than of law; and I cannot help thinking, in looking through the cases on the subject that more confusion and discrepancy have crept into them from a failure to determine precisely the facts than from any essential difference of opinion upon the abstract propositions of law, applicable to them. This seems to me notably, the case in Rumsey vs. Berry, 65 Maine, 570, where in the trial court, instead of submitting the question of fact as to what the contract really was, it not being in writing, to the jury, instructions were asked that as a matter of law the contract was a wagering contract. This instruction was properly refused, but there was a total failure to fairly submit the question of fact to the jury. It is not to be wondered at that on an appeal to the Supreme Court, the facts not being fairly determined, the opinion sustaining the transactions as legal, should have been given by a divided court, four judges concurring in the decision of the court, one judge delivering a dissenting opinion, one judge concurring in a dissentsenting opinion, and still another judge "*inclined to concur*" in it. If there had been an eighth judge it might not be improbable that he would have been "inclined to concur" in both opinions. And all this simply because the facts themselves not having been determined, there was no tangible, well defined question of law before the court.

The testimony in the case at bar is quite exhaustive and voluminous. It is confined, however, to a few points, and though somewhat conflicting, I have had no great difficulty in determining the facts to my satisfaction. It is proven that at the time these contracts were made, C. B. Stevens & Sons had not the grain on hand at DeSoto where they purchased grain, or elsewhere, nor any expectation of having it, with which to fill the contracts.

Chas. B. Stevens, the active member of the bankrupt firm, testifies that at the time he telegraphed to defendants to purchase the corn, they had not a bushel on hand, and did not expect to have any to deliver on the orders; that they were not dealing in corn at DeSoto or anywhere else, and never did, except "scalping" in it at Chicago; that they had no agreement with defendants to ship corn to fill the orders, and that the understanding was that they were merely "scalping" or option deals, and were to be settled by paying or receiving the difference at the maturity of the contract or before; that they never did deliver any corn on these sales; that defendants claimed that they bought in the options at different times and charged the difference to C. B. Stevens & Sons.

He says also, that he had no conversation with defendants until after the transactions were closed up; that he then had a talk with both of them in relation to these deals; that it was on the Board of Trade at Chicago that he asked M. H. Foss how they settled these options or "scalps," and if there was any wheat or corn delivered, and he said no; that it was done generally by forming rings among members of the Board by clerks that they employed; that these clerks settled the deals between parties in the ring whom they may have sold to or bought of, and by paying or receiving differences as the case might be; that he thinks he asked him about the delivery of grain, and he said no grain ever passed. Witness says this was the kind of transaction he was operating in, as he under-. stood it, and that no grain was to be delivered or received on these contracts, and that he understood them to be mere wagers on the future price of grain, and that defendants regarded them in the same light. That they continued this kind of deal with defendants until the fall of 1876.

On cross examination he says he commenced sending orders to defendants before he had any conversation with them; that it was a month after these transactions that he had the talk with them in Chicago; that defendants were their agents and commission merchants in Chicago; that he understood that Foss & Co. were liable for the damages for the non-fulfillment of the contracts they made for C. B. Stevens & Sons, and that they expected to make good to them the losses which they might incur in their behalf; and that if defendants failed to comply with the contracts they made for the bankrupts they would be deprived of their privileges on the Board of Trade; that Foss and he never talked about their agreement with one another in respect to these transactions, and that this conversation only related to the general course of business on the Board of Trade; that he (witness) understands that all contracts, where wheat is sold and not actually delivered, are wagering or betting contracts; and that all option contracts are betting contracts. The other Stevenses testify substantially in the same way as to their understanding of the transaction, but not as to the conversation with defendants in Chicago. And this is the substance of the testimony for the complainant. The defendants positively deny the conversation testified to by C. B. Stevens. They swear, in substance, that they had no understanding about these contracts different from what might be inferred from what appears on the face of the transaction itself; that they were executed in their usual course of business in the same manner that all the business on the Board of Trade relating to option contracts for future delivery of grain is transacted; that instead of understanding that no wheat or corn was to be delivered, their understanding was just the contrary; that the grain must be delivered according to the terms of the contract in all cases; that there was no option in the matter except as to the day in November on which the delivery was to be made; that if not delivered before, it must at all events be delivered on the last day of the month; they did not know whether Stevens & Sons had the grain to ship from DeSoto, and did not stop to inquire, but supposed they might have it ; that if they did not ship it, they (Foss & Co.) were bound to deliver the grain for them; that the contracts, according to universal custom on the Board of Trade, were made in the name of S. D. Foss & Co.; the name of their customer not being disclosed to the other party or ever inquired after. They testify that they have never dealt in what are called " puts" and " calls," such as are described *in re* Chandler, 9 N. B. R., 514, and that such contracts, which give the opinion to deliver or receive; or not, are prohibited by the rules of the Board of Trade as well as by the laws of Illinois; that they made these contracts with various members of the Board of Trade, for and on behalf of the bankrupts at their request, and on their behalf, and for their benefit, in entire good faith, without any understanding that they were not to be performed, and that Stevens & Sons not shipping the grain they performed their contracts by going upon the market and purchasing the wheat and corn ; that as to 30,000 bushels of corn they made a delivery, and as to the balance they closed out the deal in the manner before indicated by mutual offset and adjustment of differences; that this adjustment of differences is a mere matter of convenience to the members of the Board, and to their customers; that no person is under the least obligation to settle in that way, and that dealers may and often do insist upon an actual delivery of the grain, and that settlement frequently saves to their customers the cost of insurance and storage. That the object of forming these rings or clearing houses is to close out the transactions and get them off their books; and this is what they call "*ringing it out.*" But that it frequently cannot be done in that way; as if, for any reason, one whose assistance is essential to complete the circle prefers an actual delivery in which case the ring is " burst;" and then each must perform his contract by actual delivery of the grain. Their testimony is full and fair and intelligent, upon the questions at issue, and they are corroborated by several other witnesses, ex-presidents, ex-directors, ex-commissioners of appeals, and present members of the Board of Trade and some of the persons with whom these contracts were made. The testimony is conclusive that this business was done much in the same manner that all the other business on the Board of Trade is done respecting contracts for the future delivery of grain. They all agree that there is no option except the option to deliver on any day of the month; and that the seller is bound, not only by the contract but by the rules of the board, to which it is made subject, to perform his contract by an actual delivery, unless excused from the performance by the act of the other party; and for a violation of this rule he is subject to the discipline of the board, and to be dismissed therefrom if he insists upon the violation of his contract.

Now, which party is best corroborated in their misunderstanding of the contract by the admitted facts of the case?

It is clear to me by all odds that the defendants are best corroborated.

It is very easy for either party to swear to what his own understanding of the contract was, but that standing alone is manifestly immaterial. The secret intentions of one party contrary to what appears on the face of the contract, and not communicated to the other party, cannot prevail to make a contract illegal which is otherwise valid. The real question is, what was the contract? and that implies an inquiry as to the mutual understanding and meeting of the minds of the parties. What was that? It is easy for a party to swear what his own understanding and intentions were, but when he comes to swear to the intentions and understanding of the other party, the consideration due to his testimony stands on an entirely different footing. He may be presumed to know his own intentions, but the evidence of the intentions of the other party should not be of a merely subjective character, but should consist of tangible facts and circumstances outside of his own consciousness, and a knowledge of which would be capable of satisfying other minds.

The conversation with the defendants testified to by Stevens, besides being denied by them, if proven, is not very strong evidence, for Stevens admits that this was a month after these transactions occurred, and was a general conversation relating to the general manner of doing business upon the board, and not to the transactions in question. But aside from the testimony as to this conversation what is there in the case to show that S. D. Foss & Co. had any intention in regard to these contracts different from what is fairly evidenced by the contracts and transactions themselves as they appear upon their face? The telegrams were orders in writing, and gave positive directions to sell grain; not to sell a privilege to deliver or not. The evidence shows at the time they were made there had been no previous communications or understandings in regard to these purchases. When received Foss & Co. went upon the market and executed the orders by making written contracts of which the following is a blank copy, or verbal contracts to the same effect:

"GRAIN CONTRACT. CHICAGO, —, 1874.

"We have this day sold A. B. & Co. ten thousand bushels of No. 2 corn, in store at ——— cents per bushel, to be delivered at sellers' option, during the month of November, 1874, ——— in lots of 5,000

bushels each.   This contract is subject in all respects to the rules and
regulations of the Board of Trade of the city of Chicago.
   " M — at — cts.

" S. D. Foss & Co.
" Per ————."

   When these contracts matured the defendants performed them by a
delivery of the grain, except when by the mutual arrangement of the
parties concerned the contracts were taken up and canceled, and then
they invariably paid in cash the damages which the law would have
obliged them to pay upon a failure to perform their agreement; that is to
say, the difference between the contract price and the market price on
the day when delivery should have been made.

   Now, in the absence of more convincing testimony, what the parties
actually did is pretty good evidence of what they intended to do; and I
must conclude that upon the face of the transaction as shown by the acts
and conduct of the parties, the evidence is very strong that these sales
were *bona fide* sales, and not made with any intent, *mutual between the
parties*, to violate the law.

   The notes and mortgage sought to be set aside (as well as the
original contracts for the sale of the grain, both as between the bankrupts
and S. D. Foss & Co., and between S. D. Foss & Co. and the parties with
whom they contracted), being in writing and perfectly fair on their face,
and given for a full money consideration without any pretense of fraud or
unfair dealing, the burden of making a clear case for setting them aside
for illegality lies with the complainant.   There should be in his favor a
clear preponderance in the weight of the evidence: Pixley *vs.* Boynton,
79 Ill., 351.   Contracts made and so deliberately entered into upon adequate consideration, without fraud, should not be set aside for light or
transient reasons, or mere suspicion of being contrary to law.   But instead of there being a preponderance of proofs in favor of the complainant, I am obliged to believe that the weight of evidence is the other
way, and I must find as facts:

   1. That C. B. Stevens & Sons, when they gave the orders for the
sale of the grain, had no grain to deliver, no contracts made by which
they expected to obtain it, and no expectation of ever having it delivered
by shipping to the defendants.

   They did expect and intend, however, that S. D. Foss & Co.
would make these contracts much as they did, in fact, make them, and
that they would, at their maturity, take care of them for C. B. Stevens

& Sons in about the same manner they did take care of them, by a delivery of the grain or by a settlement and adjustment of the differences according to circumstances; and that whatever the profits were, they were to be credited with them, and if there were losses, such losses were to be borne by them.

2. That the defendants did not know that C. B. Stevens & Sons had not the grain, but had no reason to expect that they had or would obtain it to ship to Chicago in sufficient amounts to fill the orders, but intended that if C. B. S. & Sons did not ship the grain, they (defendants) would perform their contracts with the parties with whom they were severally made in C. B. Stevens & Sons behalf, in good faith, by a delivery of the grain, unless delivery was dispensed with by the parties who had a right to insist upon a fulfillment of the contract, and that there was no mutual understanding that the contracts were mere wagers on the price of grain for the November market, or that there was to be, in fact, no delivery, but only an adjustment of differences.

3. The understanding of the other parties to these contracts, to whom sales were made, as to their being performed, was the same as that of the defendants.

Having determined the facts, the law applicable to the case is not difficult.

1. The contracts sought to be set aside are written contracts, and the mortgage is under seal. Nevertheless, the weight of authority, and I think that of doctrine, is, that you shall go behind the writing and show what the real intent and meaning of the parties were; and if it appears that the writing does not express the real intent of the parties, but is merely colorable, and used as a cloak to cover a gambling transaction, the court will not lend its aid to enforce the contract, however fair on its face; or if securities are given, as in this case, will interfere on grounds of public policy and for the public good rather than for the purpose of relieving a party who is himself *particeps criminis* in an inhibited transaction, to set aside such securities: *In re* John Green, 65 U. B. R., 198, and the cases there cited.

2. A contract for the future delivery of personal property, which the seller has not got when the contract is made, nor any means of getting it, is not void for illegality.

That was held in Porter *vs.* Viets, 1 Bissell, 177, and is the settled law. See Logan *vs.* Musick and Brown, 81 Ill., 415; Hibblewhite *vs.* McMorine, 5 Meeson and Welsby, 462.

The seller is bound by the contract to deliver the goods, and if he fails must pay damages.

Such contracts, though entered into for pure purposes of speculation, however censurable when made by those engaged in ordinary mercantile pursuits, and who have creditors dependent for the pay of their just claims upon their prudent management in business, are nevertheless not prohibited by law.

As said in Porter vs. Viets, *supra*, "People might differ about the propriety of making such a contract by one who did not know certainly where he was to acquire the property, but having made it, the courts will compel him to abide by it." That case was on demurrer, and was in many essential respects similar to the one at bar.

The substance of the contract itself is what must control. The secret intention of one of the parties uncommunicated to the other party, not to fulfill his contract, is not enough to make the transaction illegal. The intent that it should be a mere betting upon the market, without any expectation of actual performance, must be mutual and constitute an integral part of the real contract, in order to vitiate it.

Furthermore, supposing it had been the mutual intention of S. D. Foss & Co. and the bankrupts that these contracts were not to be performed, I do not see that that would make them illegal, so long as the other parties to the contract did not participate in that illegal intention. S. D. Foss & Co. and C. B. Stevens & Sons did not constitute the parties to the contract. There was no contract for the sale and delivery of grain made between them. As between them the relation existed of principal and agent. S. D. Foss & Co. made the contract in their own name, but for and in behalf of C. B. Stevens & Sons, and S. D. Foss & Co. and and C. B. Stevens & Sons constitute but one party to the contract, whether it be considered as a contract between S. D. Foss & Co. and the parties in Chicago with whom they dealt, or as a contract between C. B. Stevens & Sons and those same parties; and there is no evidence whatever to show that those other parties had any notice or knowledge of this gambling intent. On the contrary, they knew that Foss & Co., as the evidence shows, and some of these same parties testify, were men of high standing and responsibility on the Board of Trade, and would perform their agreements; Leehman Bros. vs. Strassberger, 2 Woods C. C. R., 554, and Wolcott vs. Heath, 78 Ill., 433, are directly in point.

4. If the original contracts for the sale of grain were liable to the taint of illegality, as charged, it does not necessarily follow that the notes

and mortgage executed by one of the principals in the transaction to secure the payment of moneys previously advanced by their agent to pay losses springing out of, and resulting from, those original transactions, are contaminated with the same vice.

This question is fairly presented by this record, though the decision of the point is not necessary to the case, and I do not care to decide it. I shall, therefore, content myself with referring to some few high authorties, which hold such a contract valid. The leading English case, decided by Lord Mansfield, is Falkney vs. Renous, 4 Burr, 2,069. Following this are Petrie vs. Hanway, 3 Term. Rep., 418; Farmer vs. Russell, 1 Bos. & Pull., 296.

The first case cited is a strong case, and though seemingly questioned by Lord Kenyon in Petrie vs. Hanway, *supra*, has never been overruled, I believe, in England. Marshall, C. J., cites it approvingly in Armstrong vs. Toler, 11 Wheat, 258. See, also, Owen vs. Davis, 1 Baily, s. c., 315, and the recent case before cited of Lehman vs. Strassberger, 2 Woods, C. C. R., 554, which is very much in point, I think. This, I believe, is undoubtedly the result of the English cases. How far the rule has been changed by statute, or by decisions in the several states, I do not care to inquire.

5. Whatever might be the judgment of discreet men as to the propriety of such purely speculative transactions as are disclosed by this record, undertaken by men in mercantile pursuits, I am unable to see, on general principles, any objection to them in point of law. The law does not undertake to prevent speculation. It does not undertake the Quixotic task of nicely governing men in all the relations of life, and compelling them to do, under all circumstances, what is prudent and reasonable. The truth is, men are speculating creatures as certainly as they are eating and sleeping ones. And, although it is undoubtedly true that much harm comes to the community from over speculation, it is more than doubtful if the world would be better off without speculators; or, if it would be, that the law can do much in the way of abolishing them.

As a common thing, business men are prone to regard their own judgment of the market as a part of their capital, and to a certain extent they have a right so to do.

It is only with the more manifest abuses of the privileges of citizens in their dealings with one another, and when the evil touches and infects the public welfare, that the law assumes to interfere. In the main, commercial transactions must be left to be regulated by the higher and more

inexorable laws which govern the trading world. . If the transactions disclosed by this case are illegal, then undoubtedly a great part of the
banking and clearing house transactions in our great commercial centers
are illegal also.

I am persuaded that to hold them so would be trenching too severely upon the business of the commercial world, without any corresponding benefit to be expected from it.

It might be a difficult task to lay down any single rule or draw a
straight line which should define or divide all merely speculative from
all pure gambling transactions, for it must be admitted that the same
prime element of risk is common to both. But it has seemed to me that
according to any reasonable rule which it would be practicable to enforce, these transactions must fall in the side of legal speculations. They
were carried on in good faith, and in the usual and ordinary course of
business upon the Board of Trade, which it seems undertakes to exercise
a salutary control over its members, it appearing in evidence that if any
member fails or refuses to perform his contract by delivery or receiving
grain which he has agreed to deliver or receive, he is subject to the discipline of that body; and if the offending member is still refractory or
contumacious, he is suspended or finally dismissed from the Board, thus
adding to the penalties which the law attaches to a violation of contracts,
the sanction of a wholesome family discipline. The witnesses agree that
what are called "puts" and "calls" are not allowed to members of the
Board, and that "scalpers" cannot live in that atmosphere, they bearing
the same relation to that fraternity of commercial gentlemen that shysters do to full-bred lawyers. If that be so, certainly they are far enough
asunder.

Then again, if we look at the equities of this case, aside from the
special head of equity, under which the court, in the interest of the public good, will interfere to set aside and cancel securities given upon a
gaming consideration, the general equities and intrinsic justice of the
case are largely with the defendants. The whole business was originated and carried on at the instance and for the benefit of the bankrupts.
Whatever of legal turpitude attaches to these transactions, it is evident
that C. B. Stevens & Sons were not merely *particeps criminis*, but the
principal offenders. When profits ensued, as they frequently did, they
put them down in their own pockets. On one occasion it is in evidence
that they represented to defendants that they had made quite large
amounts, something like $10,000 out of these deals. Why, then, if it

was their deal, and they enjoyed the profits when there were profits, should they not bear the loses when the market turned against them, and these fell to their lot, and not shuffle them off upon their agents who, it is not denied, had acted fairly and honorably with them?

Foss & Co. had no interest in these transactions, except their commissions, and instead of leading the bankrupts on in this business, the evidence of the bankrupts is that they discouraged them on every occasion. Their letters, introduced in evidence by the complainant, show that S. D. Foss & Co., from time to time, dissuaded the bankrupts from these speculating deals—told them they were taking too much risk, both in respect to wheat and corn; that there was a small stock of old corn in the market, that the new crop had not yet been moved, that there was danger of a "corner" being run, and sending prices up, and on one occasion protested that if they insisted upon taking such risks they must employ other commission men. These letters were relied upon to show that these defendants understood these deals to be gambling transactions; but to my mind they simply show a proper appreciation, on the part of the defendants, of the risks which men, in the circumstances and business of the bankrupts, were taking on themselves, and a due consideration for the interests of their principals in that behalf. But C. B. Stevens & Sons, relying confidently on their own judgment and sources of knowledge, as men are inclined to do, continued the business until the tide turned against them. Under these circumstances, one would say that the commonest kind of honesty that passes current among men should require C. B. Stevens & Sons to pay these losses, and not shift them off upon their factors. Of course the assignee stands, as far as legal right goes, in no better case than the bankrupts; and it is due to the bankrupts to say that, as far as they are personally concerned, they have never objected to the payment of these claims, though they are now the main witnesses for the claimant, and in their testimony say they want him to succeed. The assignee, of course, in the interest of the creditors, has only done his duty in bringing these matters before the court for adjudication.

I have not undertaken to review the decisions upon this subject. I have not thought it essential. Those of the highest tribunal in Illinois, though not perhaps entirely reconcilable, I think are so in the main, and go to support the transaction disclosed by the case at bar. Whatever the discrepancy there is, as I have before remarked, arises more from the facts than from the law. The most that can be said is, that different courts have come to different conclusions upon different state of facts. This cannot be wondered at, and is unavoidable. How far the judgment of the court, in a given case upon the facts, may be influenced by its opinion of the law and the essential justice of the case, cannot always be known. I confess I have a strong predilection in favor of holding men of full age and right mind to their contracts deliberately entered into upon full and adequate money considerations, without deceit or imposition, and when the consequences of their contracts, however ill-advised, are mainly personal to themselves.

I think the case cited of Wolcott vs. Heath, 78 Ill., 433, Pixley vs. Boynton, 79 Ill., 351, and Logan vs. Musick, 81 Ill., 426, express the law of that state on the subject, and are authorities in the case at bar.

The case of Lyon vs. Culbertson, reported in 9 Chicago Legal News 185, Feb. 24, 1874, and Vol. 5, No. 19, p. 401 of the Central Law Journal, in which Justice Dickey delivers a vigorous dissenting opinion, I am told, was decided before the cases in the 79th and 81st Ill. Reports. However that may be, and whether the decision be good law or not, I do not see that it is necessarily at variance with the other cases, nor that it attempts to overrule or qualify them in the least.

That seemed to turn on a question that is not presented in this case.

There is no failure to perform, or offer to perform, on the part of S. D. Foss & Co. on any of the contracts which they made; nor anything in the contracts dispensing with an offer to perform.

Again, it must be incontestible, that if the contracts were valid in their inception, and not tainted with any gambling intent or device, a subsequent mutual settlement by the parties, which took the place of actual performance, cannot have the retroactive effect of making them void for illegality. If the contracts were void at all, they must have been void when made. The subsequent conduct of the parties may, and should, be considered as evidence tending to show what the real contracts were when entered into; but if they were originally valid, no subsequent act of the parties can have the effect to render them obnoxious to the taint of illegality as being gambling contracts.

I have not overlooked the case of In re Green, supra, decided by my learned and lamented predecessor; 15 B. R., 198.

I have not had occasion to review the evidence from which the conclusions of fact in that case were drawn, and it is enough to say that upon the findings of the fact made, the law is undoubtedly correctly stated. Bill dismissed.

THE "ANTI-CORNER RULE."

The attempt to repeal the so-called "Anti-Corner" rule of the Chicago Board of Trade has elicited diverse opinions from interested parties as to the merits or demerits of said rule, demonstrating the truth of the aphorism, "many men of many minds." Still, despite conflicting opinions and arguments upon the subject, it must be conceded that the weight of argument is most decidedly in favor of some rule that will effectually prevent corners as they frequently occurred in former years, and as they are certain to occur under a system which allows the purchaser of property to fix his own measure of damages in case of default.

The object and intent of the rule in question was to discountenance the formation of "Corners" on unwarrantably manipulated and fictitious markets, by protecting as far as might be, those who were caught short or who for any reason were unable to specifically fulfill their contracts.

This rule has worked satisfactorily in the main for some three years; it gives every operator a fair show in the field, and insures to all, a realization of all legitimate profits in their deals. There is some limit to exactions and the extortionate crowd are kept within reasonable bounds. As a matter of course, it is impracticable to frame rules requiring infinitely varied application which will not occasionally work hardship; but it is probable if the rule under consideration were abolished, there would be twenty sufferers where there is now one.

The principal objection to the rule as it stands is not in any hardship that has ever occurred by its application, but in the persistent misinterpretation of its provisions. In many instances outside parties have been induced to sell short, on the assurance from their commission merchants that under this rule they could default on their contracts with impunity, and that the measure of damages, if any, would be determined on the basis of the value of the property for shipment to Eastern markets; whereas the rule provides that as only one of the elements in determining its value, and no such simple question in arithmetic has ever been applied as a finality in the decision of any case under the rule. The local demand occasioned by rules made in excess of the supply at the maturity of contracts will probably be always more or less considered in determining the real current value of property. Such prices may be entirely legitimate, and not in any sense the result of combination or partaking in any degree of extortion—they are not fictitious in any sense and are not under the provisions of the rule to be disregarded. Purely fictitious prices are and ought to be repudiated, and such undoubtedly are those paid for or bid by a party or combination merely for the purpose of establishing values on a basis that will enable them to extort money damages from those unable to specifically fulfill their engagements.

That a great majority of the legitimate receivers and dealers are opposed to a return to the former rule in this respect is unquestionable, and actually believe it would encourage dishonesty and give rise to uncertainty; that there would be no stability in prices, and all concerned, whether merchants, producers or shippers, would be at the mercy of unprincipled and irresponsible sharpers, who would bring the Board of Trade and the city into disrepute and disgrace. Honor would be at a ruinous discount, and integrity would be as a foot-ball kicked hither and yon by every shyster.

The inevitable effect of corners is demoralizing to individuals and damaging to the interests of legitimate trade, and is forbidden by the laws of England so far back that the memory of man runneth not to the contrary. The July corner, as statistics plainly show, caused an immense falling off. of both domestic and foreign shipments of grain, and the practical embargo was seriously felt by a score of interests. Moreover, such a condition of things has a decided tendency to permanently injure our foreign grain trade by turning orders into other channels.

Some parties argue that the Anti-Corner rule serves to depress the market and give the advantage to other points, but this will always work in consonance with the law of average, and what is apparently lost at one time will be gained at another. It is still further contended that in selling short on futures the "scalpers" should suffer. So they surely will in the long run. Did not the shorts get squeezed sufficiently in July of the present year in Chicago? We should say that ten to fifteen cents per bushel premium was ample penalty for the "crime."

Look at Milwaukee without a corner rule, where wheat was run up, say about twenty-five cents above value for Eastern shipment at the close of the month in question. Such would have been impossible had a similar rule been in operation at that point; and that the market was forced up to a fictitious figure is manifest from the tremendous tumble that ensued when the July deal had closed. And was Milwaukee benefited in the least by the disreputable business? It must have been superb fun for the mourners to see one lucky fellow take the whole pot and then hear the shout like "a rebel brigade or a million Sioux," as the report puts it, "McGeogh has won! McGeogh has won!" "Hurrah for Mac!" "Milwaukee's credit is sustained!"

Elegant past-time, this, for the victims of the Milwaukee July deal! The hero of the hour had "strictly complied with the rules of the Chamber," and the shorts must toe the mark, even if it took the bread from their children's mouths, and then have the glorious satisfaction and consolation of knowing that "Milwaukee's credit is sustained!"

The credit of Milwaukee, forsooth! Her credit and that of the Chamber of Commerce in this regard is the credit which professional gamblers may justly claim, for there is a dubious sort of "honor among thieves."

Their appears to be every good reason why the Anti-Corner rule should be sustained and abided by. The interests of the legitimate trade and fair dealing demand it, while, on the contrary, as experience has conclusively demonstrated, all corner transactions are incalculably detrimental to the moral and commercial welfare of the community.

In substantiation of the foregoing arguments against corners there is voluminous testimony. A few significant illustrations may be aptly cited herewith.

There was the memorable corner in oats of June, 1872, which proved most disastrous in every way, to every public interest. For some time it laid an embargo upon trade, and so clogged the wheels of business and choked the avenues and arteries of commerce, that the movement of all kinds of produce, of property transported by rail or water, was checked and at last, for a time, actually stopped.

On this point there is overwhelming proof, and we make a few brief extracts from the depositions of members of the Board of Trade, in the matter of Chandler, Pomeroy & Co., bankrupts, heard before Judge Blodgett in the U. S. District Court for the Northern District of Illinois, setting forth the "ways that are dark" in such transactions.

Charles Randolph, Secretary of the Board of Trade, testified that "the idea of a corner is to buy more property and contract for more property than there is available for delivery. The party must have contracts for more than there is here or can be here during the life of the contract. *Corners disorganize trade, and are very apt to disorganize the party who is running them.*"

Quite as emphatic is the testimony of Murray Nelson, who said: "I

should say corners were injurious, inasmuch as they derange trade and
commerce, force it out of its natural course, and tend to create a fictitious state of things. An undue and unusual supply is forced upon the
market without a corresponding demand within a limited space of time,
which clogs and interferes with trade in a natural way for a considerable
time afterward. Then they are very likely—almost sure—to result in
disaster, to one side inevitably, and very likely to both, *as it is decidedly
and entirely a gambling operation.*"

H. C. Ranney testified: "The effect of a corner in grain is disastrous. It unsettles prices, and destroys confidence in general trading in
grain in Chicago. The effect is disastrous on general legitimate traders
—always is, and always must be. *The corner crippled great masses of
our commission merchants very badly.*"

The late Wm. F. Coolbaugh testified: "My observation and experience of the effects of all the combinations that have been made since I
have been in business, as a banker, to corner any description of grain,
has satisfied me that they are very injurious to trade, and in all respects
demoralizing to the commercial public." He further said: "I have seen
the effect of such operations illustrated by a decline of forty cents a
bushel in wheat in twenty-four hours; ten or fifteen on oats. That illus-
trates it better than anything else."

Charles E. Culver, then President of the Board, testified: "The result of grain corners is usually disastrous to the parties interested—those
directly interested, either as buyers or sellers."

Robert Harris, Superintendent of the C. B. & Q. R. R., testified:
"The idea in a corner seems to be that there is no exchange of commodities; in other words, *it is a modern species of gambling.* The great objection to it is in that part of it which is essentially gambling, by which
an individual gets an advantage without having rendered an equivalent."

Much other evidence of a similar tenor was submitted in connection
with that "celebrated case," but enough has been given to fully corroborate our position.

As another forcible illustration of the pernicious effects of corners,
our attention has been called to the fact that in the spring of 1876, a corner (or at least an attempt to control the market) was run in No. 2 spring
wheat in this market. The parties manipulating the market were said to
have made much money, notwithstanding the fact that upon the culmin-
ation of the corner, they had on hand a large quantity of wheat. Rather
than ship this wheat, say 300,000 bushels, or sell it at value for shipment,

the parties held it until those in the trade doubted its sound condition, when it became almost unsalable. The entire wheat trade of Chicago was prostrated—the price of No. 2 spring declining to 85 cents per bushel. Trade was diverted from this city. Exporters and Eastern buyers were warned as to the quality of our wheat, and Western shippers would not ship here, for the reason that the poor wheat here dragged down to its own level the price of the good.

It was not until after such wheat was declared to be hot and out of condition, and non-deliverable on contracts for No. 2 spring wheat, that consumers and exporters dare send orders here, and country shippers felt safe to make consignments of good wheat to this market. The direct and indirect injury to the commercial interests of this city growing out of this single corner transaction is beyond computation.

Evidence of a similar character, going to illustrate the evils and disastrous results of corners, could be multiplied indefinitely, but sufficient has already been presented to convince every one that it is a practice which should be universally discountenanced and condemned, as being inimical to the interests of the business community.

A WORD OF CAUTION TO "SHORT SELLERS."

It is an error to suppose that under the rules of the Board of Trade, sellers can with impunity default in delivering property which they have sold, or have contracted to deliver. The tenor and spirit of the rules are that contracts must be fulfilled by actual delivery of property, unless previous to their maturity, they have been closed or settled. If margins are deposited as required a contract cannot be settled or closed before maturity, without consent of both parties to it, except by actual delivery of property, made in accordance with the rules. Rule xxvi, provides "in case any property for future delivery is not delivered at maturity of contract, the *purchaser* may at his option declare the contract forfeited; *or he may purchase the property on the market for account of the seller by one o'clock of the next business day*, notifying him at once of such purchase; or he may require a settlement with the seller at the average market price on the day of the maturity of the contract."

A subsequent section provides that the forgoing "shall not be construed as authorizing unjust or unreasonable claims based upon manipulated or fictitious markets. The rules further provide that in case of disputes the committee of arbitration in determining the legitimate value of pruperty shall consider its value in other markets, or for manufacturing purposes in this market, together with such other facts as, may justly enter into the determination of its true value, irrespective of any fictitious price it may at the time be selling for in this market. Provided, that in case of default on contracts for future delivery, if it shall not be shown that the seller had provided by previous purchase of the property for delivery on his contract, he shall, in the judgment of the committee, be liable to pay as penalty for such default, damage, not exceeding five (5) per cent. of the value of the property sold. From the rules quoted it will be noticed that they are designed not only to prevent "corners," but are as well calculated to prevent selling the market down on the last day of the month for the purpose of establishing a low average market as a basis for the settlement of contracts. Corners are not only to be avoided, but their converse is to be prevented as well. The plain object of the rules is to insure to buyers the delivery of property purchased for shipment, for consumption, or for other legitimate purposes, and to force the seller to provide for the specific fulfillment of his contract. We should mention, that since in force, said rules have been construed by the Committee of Arbitration as much as possible in favor of the buyer and parties who have defaulted in their deliveries, have been made to pay damages to the full extent permitted by the rule.

DEALS OF THE CURBSTONE BROKERS.

COMMONLY CALLED

"PUTS AND CALLS."

We have on preceding pages given a detailed explanation of the reprehensible business of operating by means of "Puts and Calls." But as there is a crowd of outsiders whose only occupation it would appear, is to engage in this disreputable vocation, we desire to make further remarks thereupon. Honorable, conscientious, reliable dealers and operators are averse to this illegitimate mode of doing business. It is the touch of pitch that defileth. This business is managed and manipulated chiefly by those who have lost their moral courage and have sought refuge in this demoralizing and nefarious business, where there is but a gleam of a chance, or a delusive hope of making a hit. Together with shysters, green-cloth gentry and fleecers generally. The occupation is so thoroughly that of a gamester that anybody possessing a "five spot" from a pimp to a professor may try his luck at the game. On the court adjoining, and under the shadow of the stately Chamber of Commerce building these "operators" "run the mill"—a motley assemblage of broken-down merchants, sleek "fellers" of the town, collapsed clerks, desperate "borrowers," who are striving to "make it good" by a lucky deal, callow youths with their week's wages, anxious to invest in a "put," and a very small sprinkling of respectable men who look ashamed of the company they are in. 'Tis, indeed, not a scene for a painter, but for a whitewasher or a calciminer.

There from morning till night they shout and shuffle, figure and fulminate, wager and wriggle,—do they deal in grain or produce? Not a bit of it. These "puts" are simply the private agreements by men of small means; of those who wish to speculate but are really unable to either buy or sell, and so use these engagements as a wagering insurance policy —to cover what they call their "deals" The price at which the party issuing such tickets is either above the true price or supposed value of the grain, in case the privilege is to buy of him, or below that value as he estimates it, in case it is a privilege to sell to him, the price being dependent upon the length of the period for which it is given, or the time

of year, and, of course, upon the opinions of the party as to that value,
and as to the chances of the rise or fall of the price of the commodity.

The "put" will be converted into a contract ; in other words, the
"privilege" to take or to deliver will be claimed, only in the contingency
that the seller of the "put" is mistaken about the future price of the
grain about which he has made this wager, and then the successful gamester may assert his "privilege;" then the contract is born, and may be adjusted by the payment of differences, and this is the usual way; or, it
may be broken, and then the differences are ascertained by a resale, and
thus adjusted. This *modus operandi* was formerly in vogue on the regular Board, but it is not now recognized or permitted, nor any transactions
resulting from "Puts and Calls," in fact such operations are in direct violation of the statutes of the State. To such an extent, does this custom
go that, notwithstanding the business of the greatest of grain markets is
conducted upon the Board, and immense quantities of the actual grain
are there bought and sold, for consumption, for shipment, for legitimate
speculation, by legitimate contracts, yet it is a fact that not exceeding one
in ten, and probably not one in a hundred of the contracts there made is
wound up by the delivery of the grain; but so great is this speculative
movement, that sometimes the amount *of a given grain is bought and
sold during a day*, that it actually encroaches upon the amount which
comes to the market during the season, and the actual business of a Board
professing to deal in grain is well represented as resembling a bank
"clearing house," in which the differences are ascertained, adjusted, and
divided in money; in which the contracts are consumated not by the delivery of the grain, but by the payment of the money, found to be the
differences upon the wagering contracts touching grain between the several gamesters.

To the credit of the Board, be it said, there are but very few members who deal in these "puts," which have been the means of bringing
moral and financial ruin upon so many men who once stood high in the
confidence and esteem of the community, but these few are by that number too many, and they ought to be "sat down on" by the Board. . Let it
entirely clear its skirts of the abomination, and relegate to the outside
all such infamous business transactions. Such matters would not only
trample upon the dignity, but sully the good name of the Board. The
Board should therefore *jealously* and *zealously* guard its reputation. The
whole thing is disgraceful and demoralizing. How many a poor, soul-
racked, conscience-smitten fugitive from justice can trace the beginning

of his downfall to speculations of this character. At first they hazard but small amounts, and cautiously. But they soon launch out more boldly and become servile to the infatuation. More money must be had, and in an evil moment the funds of the institution or business house with which the doomed speculator is connected are "borrowed," but never returned. The inevitable denouement is, discovery, flight, disgrace and irretrievable ruin. One of the worst features of this disreputable business is, that many honest men are insidiously demoralized by it. The disposition of men who have been unfortunate and unsuccessful in their legitimate transactions, or who have met with financial reverses, is to go into some speculative scheme with the object in view to retrieve their shattered fortunes. They have chararacteristic compunctions against "bucking the tiger" outright, in fact, they have no knowledge of such "tricks that are vain." But they have heard of fabulous wealth acquired by speculating in grain, and are tempted to try their luck just once in this direction. It may be, they think, that the fickle geddess will favor them and give them a lift that will bring them right out of their embarrasment. Cajoling themselves with the idea that it is not downright gambling, but only a little harmless speculation, requiring no great judgment or experience, they scrape together all the money they can raise and "spank it up" for a "privilege." They are disappointed in the result; it doesn't "pan out" as they hoped. But they are in a desperate strait and are determined to hazard the throw just once more. Perhaps in so doing they get something back, and now flatter themselves that their luck has turned .So they go on step by step, getting in deeper and deeper, and in their reckless desperation sacrificing everything they can lay their hands on, finding in the end that they have nothing but dead-sea fruit, which turns to ashes in the grasp!

Now, if these same men had stuck to their legitimate business and shown true moral courage in buffeting the waves of adversity, instead of rushing into this ruinous speculation, they would have been far more likely to get a firm financial footing again than by taking their chances in the arena of the gamesters. This speculative mania seems to have seized upon thousands of people. Honorable, legitimate trading becomes distasteful to them. The slow and sure "old-fashioned" methods of doing business are too tedious and irksome. They are crazy to get rich speedily. They expect something for nothing, but find, alas! that they get nothing for something. When will men learn that, whatever their pecuniary circumstances may be, the "good old way of accumulating means by honest, straightforward, persistent effort and labor is the right and only sure road to competence?

RULES GOVERNING THE INSPECTION OF GRAIN

IN THE CITY OF CHICAGO.

In force from and after August 10, 1877.

The following are the rules adopted by the Board of Railroad and Warehouse Commissioners, establishing a standard of grades for the inspection of grain, under the authority of the State of Illinois:

WINTER WHEAT.

No. 1 *White Winter Wheat* shall be pure White Winter Wheat, sound, plump, and well cleaned.

No. 2 *White Winter Wheat* shall be pure White Winter Wheat, sound and reasonably clean.

No. 1 *Red Winter Wheat* shall be pure Winter Wheat, red, or red and white mixed, sound, plump, and well cleaned.

No. 2 *Red Winter Wheat* shall be pure Winter Wheat, red, or red and white mixed, sound, and reasonably clean.

Amber Wheat, Nos. 1 and 2, shall include the lighter colored varieties of Red Wheat; quality and condition to be equal to the present standard of Nos. 1 and 2 Red Winter Wheat.

No. 3 *Winter Wheat* shall include Winter Wheat not clean and plump enough for No. 2, and weighing not less than 54 pounds to the measured bushel.

Rejected Winter Wheat shall include Winter Wheat damp, musty, or from any cause so badly damaged as to render it unfit for No. 3.

SPRING WHEAT.

No. 1 *Hard Spring Wheat* shall be sound, plump, and well cleaned.

No. 2 *Hard Spring Wheat* shall be sound, reasonably clean and of good milling quality.

No. 1 *Spring Wheat* shall be sound, plump and well cleaned.

No. 2 *Spring Wheat* shall be sound, reasonably clean, and of good milling quality.

No. 3 *Spring Wheat* shall include all inferior, shrunken or dirty Spring Wheat, weighing not less than 53 pounds to the measured bushel.

Rejected Spring Wheat shall include Spring Wheat damp, musty, grown, badly bleached, or for any other cause which renders it unfit for No. 3.

In case of mixture of Spring and Winter Wheat, it will be called Spring Wheat, and graded according to the quality thereof.

Black Sea and Flinty Pfife Wheat shall in no case be inspected higher than No. 2, and Rice Wheat no higher than Rejected.

CORN.

No. 1 *Yellow Corn* shall be yellow, sound, dry, plump and well cleaned.

No. 1 *White Corn* shall be white, sound, dry, plump and well cleaned.

High Mixed Corn shall be three-quarters yellow and equal to No. 2 in condition and quality.

No. 2 *Corn* shall be dry, reasonably clean, but not plump enough for No. 1.

No. 2 *Kiln Dried Corn* shall be sound, plump and well cleaned. White or Yellow. All kiln dried corn not good enough for No. 2 kiln-dried shall be graded as Rejected kiln-dried Corn.

New High Mixed Corn shall be three-fourths yellow, of any age, and shall be reasonably clean, but not sufficiently dry for "High Mixed or No. 2."

New Mixed Corn may be less than three-fourths yellow, of any age, and shall be reasonably dry and reasonably clean, but not sufficiently dry for No. 2.

Rejected—All damp, dirty or otherwise badly damaged Corn shall be graded as Rejected.

OATS.

No. 1 *Oats* shall be white, sound, clean, and reasonably free from other grain.

No. 2 *White Oats* shall be three-quarters white and equal to No. 1 in all other respects.

No. 2 *Oats* shall be sound, reasonably clean, and reasonably free from other grain.

Rejected—All Oats, damp, unsound, dirty or for any other cause unfit for No. 2, shall be graded as Rejected.

RYE.

No. 1 *Rye* shall be sound, plump and well cleaned.

No. 2 *Rye* shall be sound, reasonably clean, and reasonably free from other grain.

Rejected—All Rye, damp, musty, dirty, or from any cause unfit for No. 2, shall be graded as Rejected.

BARLEY.

No. 1 *Barley* shall be plump, bright, sound, clean, and free from other grain.

No. 2 *Barley* shall be sound, bright, not plump enough for No. 1, reasonably clean and reasonably free from other grain.

Extra No. 3 Barley shall include slightly shrunken and otherwise slightly damaged Barley not good enough for No. 2.

No. 3 *Barley* shall include shrunken, or otherwise damaged Barley, weighing not less than 41 pounds to the measured bushel.

Feed Barley shall include all Barley which is damp or from any cause badly damaged or unfit for malting purposes, or which is largely mixed with other grain.

The word " new" shall be inserted in each certificate of inspection of a newly harvested crop of Oats until the 15th day of August; of Rye, until the 1st day of September; of Wheat until the 1st day of November; and of Barley until the 1st day of May of each year. This change shall be construed as establishing a new grade for the time specified, to conform in every particular to the existing grades of grain, excepting the distinctions of "new" and "old."

All grain that is warm or that is in a heating condition, or is otherwise unfit for warehousing, shall not be graded.

All Inspectors shall make their reasons for grading grain, when necessary, fully known by notations on their books. The weight alone shall not determine the grade.

Each Inspector is required to ascertain the weight per measured bushel of each lot of wheat inspected by him, and note the same in his book.

Any person who shall assume to act as an Inspector of Grain, who has not first been so appointed and sworn, shall be held to be an impostor, and shall be punished by a fine of not less than $50 nor more than $100 for each and every attempt to so inspect grain, to be recovered before a justice of the peace.

Any duly authorized Inspector of Grain, who shall be guilty of neglect of duty, or who shall knowingly or carelessly inspect or grade any grain improperly, or who shall accept any money or other consideration, directly or indirectly, for any neglect of duty or for the improper performance of any duty as Inspector of Grain, and any person who shall improperly influence any Inspector of Grain in the performance of his duties as such Inspector, shall be deemed guilty of a misdemeanor, and, on conviction, shall be fined in a sum of not less than $100 nor more than $1,000, in the discretion of the court, or shall be imprisoned in the county jail not less than three nor more than twelve months, or both, in the discretion of the court.

All Assistant Inspectors, when upon duty, shall wear a badge furnished by the Chief Inspector, plainly designating the position of each in the department.

The said Chief Inspector, and all persons inspecting grain under his direction, shall in no case make the grade of grain above that of the poorest quality found in any lot of grain when it has evidently been mixed or doctored for the purpose of deception.

All persons employed in the inspection of grain shall report all attempts to defraud the system of grain inspection as established by law. They shall also report to the said Chief Inspector, in writing, all instances where warehousemen deliver or attempt to deliver, grain of a lower grade than that called for by the warehouse receipt. They shall also report all attempts of receivers or shippers of grain to instruct or in any way influence the action or opinion of the Inspector, and the Chief Inspector shall report all such cases to the Commissioners.

RAILROAD AND WAREHOUSE COMMISSIONERS OF ILLINOIS.—Wm. M. Smith, J. H. Oberly, George M. Bogue.

CHIEF INSPECTOR OF GRAIN.—John P. Reynolds.

COMMITTEE OF APPEALS ON GRAIN INSPECTIONS.—P. W. Dater, S. D. Foss, T. H. Seymour.

AMENDMENT

To Rule Two (2) of the Rules Governing the Inspection of Grain in the City of Chicago, to take effect October 1, 1878.

RULE II.—SPRING WHEAT.

No. 1 *Hard Spring Wheat* shall be sound, plump and well cleaned.

No. 2 *Hard Spring Wheat* shall be sound, reasonably clean, and of good milling quality.

No. 1 *Spring Wheat* shall be sound, plump and well cleaned.

No. 2 *Spring Wheat* shall be sound, reasonably clean, and of good milling quality.

No. 3 *Spring Wheat* shall include all inferior, shrunken, or dirty Spring Wheat weighing not less than 53 pounds to the measured bushel.

Rejected Spring Wheat shall include Spring Wheat damp, musty, grown, badly bleached, or for any other cause which renders it unfit for No. 3.

In case of mixture of Spring and Winter Wheat it shall be called mixed Wheat, and graded according to the quality thereof. This rule shall be in force on and after Oct. 1, 1878; but it is provided that all Wheat in store on said date, inspected in as Spring Wheat under the rule hereby amended, shall be inspected out in accordance with the provisions of said rule as Spring Wheat.

Black Sea and Flinty Pfife Wheat shall in no case be inspected higher than No. 2, and Rice Wheat no higher than rejected.

W. M. SMITH,
GEORGE M. BOGUE,
JOHN H. OBERLY,
Railroad and Warehouse Commissioners.

Chicago, Ill., Sept. 6, 1878.

WEIGHTS.

Established by Law in the State of Illinois for the bushel of the follow-

ing Articles.

Articles.	Lbs.	Articles.	Lbs.
Wheat	60	Clover Seed	60
Shelled Corn	56	Timothy Seed	45
Ear Corn	70	Flax Seed	56
Oats	32	Hemp Seed	44
Rye	56	Blue Grass Seed	14
Barley	48	White Beans	60
Buckwheat	52	Castor Beans	46
Malt	38	Irish Potatoes	60
Corn Meal	48	Sweet Potatoes	55
Bran	20	Turnips	55
Dried Apples	24	Onions	57
Dried Peaches	33	Coarse Salt	50
Lime (unslacked)	80	Fine Salt	55

LAWS OF TRADE.

RATES OF INSPECTION.

GRAIN.

For inspecting grain from cars, per car..... ....$0 25
For inspecting grain from wagons, per load............................... 10
For inspecting grain aboard of vessels, per M bushels........ 40
For inspecting grain from canal boats......... 40
For inspecting grain in sacks, per bushel..................................... ½
For inspecting grain to cars, in bulk, per car.............................. 30
For inspecting grain to teams, per car.......: 30
For inspecting grain to teams, per load..... 10

FLOUR.

For inspecting flour, per barrel................................ ....$0 02
For inspecting flour, per sack.. 01

PROVISIONS.

For inspecting beef and pork—for the first five barrels, per barrel............. 1 00
For inspecting beef and pork—for each additional barrel.... 50
For inspecting bulk or boxed meats, per M pounds....................... 25
For inspecting lard, tallow and grease, per package......................... 05
For stripping lard, tallow and grease, per package,....... .... 1 00

HIGHWINES.

For inspecting highwines, per barrel....................:.................... 10

WEIGHMASTER'S TARIFF OF PRICES.

Sundries, weighed on platform and beam scales, and handled at the expense of the Weighmaster, will be charged as follows:

Grain, seed, beans, potatoes, and similar articles, in bags, per bag..... ..... $0 02
Sugar, in hogsheads and boxes, per 100 pounds........ 02
Salt, in sacks, per 100 pounds.. 02
Pig iron and lead, per 100 pounds........................ 02
Bulk or boxed meats, per 100 pounds......................... 02
Broom corn, in lots of 50 bales or more, per bale.... 06
Broom corn, in lots of less than 50 bales, per bale........ 07
Wool, per sack, in lots of 50 or more 07
Wool, per sack, in lots of less than 50....................................... 08
Coal and salt, per ton.. 05
Lard, tallow, grease and stearine, per package............................... 05
Butter and lard, in kegs, each.. 04
Dressed hogs, each.. 02
Salt, sugar, dried fruit, and similar articles, per barrel....................... 04
For weighing grain to vessels, by cargo, from elevators, per M bushels........ 25
For weighing grain from canal boats, per boat.............................. 1 00

REGULATIONS

INSPECTION OF FLOUR IN CHICAGO.

Adopted by the Board of Trade, May 21, 1878.

TO TAKE EFFECT JUNE 1, 1878.

REGULATION I.

GRADES.—The Board of Directors shall establish and fix the standards for two grades of "Super" Flour and two grades of "Extra" Flour, to be designated respectively "Fine," "Superfine," "Extra," and "Double Extra." Samples of these standards shall be furnished to the Flour Inspectors for their government in inspecting, and also to the Secretary of the Association, to be kept by him for comparison.

REGULATION II.

INSPECTION COMMITTEE.—The Board of Directors shall appoint a standing committee on Flour Inspection, to consist of five members, at least three of whom shall be dealers in Flour. Said committee shall have and exercise a general control of the Inspection of Flour.

REGULATION III.

FLOUR TO INSPECT AS SOUND —Flour classed as sound shall be strictly sound, free from any and every defect or fault, causing either smell or taste.

REGULATION IV.

FLOUR TO INSPECT AS UNSOUND.—All Flour not sound, whether the unsoundness be derived from the condition of the grain from which it was manufactured, or has originated in the Flour, shall-be classed as unsound.

REGULATION V.

INSPECTION.—The Inspectors of Flour shall inspect "Superfine" and " Extra" by grade only. "Fine" or " Double Extra" may be inspected by grade or by sample, as requested by the party ordering the inspection. Samples of all Flour inspected shall be furnished by the Inspectors to the party ordering the inspection.

REGULATION VI.

BRANDING.—The Inspectors shall brand all Flour, except that below the standard of "Fine" that has been inspected as "sound" and "full weight," and none other. For branding, stencils shall be used which shall state the month in which the Flour was inspected, and on "Superfine" and "Extra" shall also state the grade of the Flour.

REGULATION VII.

CERTIFICATES OF INSPECTION.—Certificates of Inspection shall be issued only as "Superfine" or " Extra" on all Flour so graded. Certificates may be issued by grade or by sample, as desired by the party ordering the inspection, on any Flour inspecting " Double Extra" " Fine" or below " Fine;" but when issued by grade the Flour shall be branded as of the grade. No certificate shall be issued for part of any lot of Flour inspected, without the consent of both the buyer and seller. When Flour is unsound, the Inspectors shall state in their certificates the character of the unsoundness, as *musty, hard sour, soft sour,* or *slightly unsound,* (the latter qualification of the unsoundness being intended to indicate that the Flour will probably work sound for immediate use, and is but slightly depreciated in value,) the number of packages of each description, and also, when practicable, the number of packages that may be so stained or out of condition as to depreciate the market value of the Flour. In case the Flour has been overhauled and cleaned on account of having been wet, and the Inspectors shall deem such overhauling in any way damaging to the market value of the Flour, they shall note on their certificates "wet and cleaned." If Flour is in flat-hooped barrels the Inspectors shall so note in their certificates.

REGULATION VIII.

Re-Inspection.—When on re-inspection Flour is found to be sour, it shall be re-weighed, but no charge shall be made by the Inspectors for weighing, if it proves to be short in weight.

REGULATION IX.

Weights.—A barrel of Flour shall be deemed to weigh one hundred and ninety-six (196) pounds net, and no allowance shall be made for any overweight. In case of short weights, the buyer shall be allowed for the shortage at the rate he pays and one-half a cent per pound on the same for freight, and in addition five (5) cents per barrel for the expense of refilling. Buyers of sacked Flour shall be allowed reclamation for short weights only. The Inspectors shall satisfy themselves in regard to weights, and in case they deem it necessary to strip some of the Flour, they shall strip (5) barrels from each lot, and shall be entitled to fifteen (15) cents for each barrel so stripped; if it proves to be short in weight, the charge for stripping to be paid by the seller.

REGULATION X.

Inspector's Fees.—The fee for inspecting and branding Flour shall be two (2) cents per barrel, and for Flour in sacks one (1) cent per sack.

REGULATION XI.

Irregular Flour.—When Flour inspects "Double Extra," "Fine" or below "Fine," or when the Inspectors are working to a sample, in case the Flour does not run uniform, the Inspectors shall note that fact on their certificates, together with the number of packages of each quality, samples of which shall be submitted to the party ordering the inspection for examination.

REGULATION XII.

FURTHER DUTIES OF INSPECTORS.—It shall be the duty of Inspectors to furnish the standard samples of Flour to which they are working to the Committee on Flour Inspection, for the use of the Secretary of the Association, monthly or oftener if directed, and also to keep in their office, for the accommodation of the trade, the official standard samples of "Double Extra," "Extra," "Superfine," and "Fine" Flour in current use in New York, Boston, Philadelphia, Baltimore, St. Louis and Montreal; said samples to be furnished by the Secretary of the Association. It shall be the further duty of the Inspectors to ascertain the stock of Flour in Chicago on the first day of each month, and to report the same to the Secretary of the Association, to be by him posted upon the bulletin of the Exchange room. In taking the account of stock there shall be included only the amount in the several freight depots, the public warehouses and the places of storage by receivers, and in the city mills. The Inspectors shall also furnish to the Secretary of the Association, monthly, a statement of the number of barrels and the number of sacks of Flour inspected by them during the preceding month, designating the amount inspected of each grade, and the amount inspected by sample.

REGULATION XIII.

LIABILITIES OF INSPECTORS.—The Inspectors shall only be liable for damages for any discrepancy between the Flour for which a certificate is issued and the sample they retain of the Flour so inspected, unless the buyer furnishes them a sample to inspect by, or the standard sample is used. In all claims for errors of inspection by grade, the final test shall be by the standard samples in the care of the Secretary of the Association.

REGULATION XIV.

All former regulations governing the inspection of Flour are hereby annulled—to take effect June 1, 1878.

COMMITTEE ON FLOUR INSPECTION FOR 1878.

N. E. PLATT, Chairman.

THOMAS HEERMANS,   I. N. ASH,   GILBERT MONTAGUE,

EDMUND NORTON.

REGULATIONS FOR THE INSPECTION OF HAY.

No. 1 Timothy—Shall be Timothy, and not more than one-fifth of other tame grasses mixed ; good color, well cured, and free from must.

No. 2 Timothy—Shall be Timothy, and not more than one-third of other tame grasses mixed ; good color, well cured, and free from must.

Mixed Hay—Shall consist of tame grasses, mixed; good color, well cured, and free from must.

Prime Prairie—Shall be purely upland Hay, free from swail grasses; good color, well cured, and free from must.

No. 1 Prairie—Shall be upland and midland Prairie Hay; good color, well cured, and free from must.

No. 2 Prairie—Shall be swail or slough Hay, either wholly or mixed with upland; good color, well cured, and free from must.

No Grade Hay—All kinds of Hay, badly cured, stained, or in any way out of condition ; the certificate of inspection stating whether it is Tame or Prairie Hay.

All Hay that is sent for inspection under the Rules of the Board shall be graded, and each separate bale marked with its respective grade immediately when taken from the car in which it is sent to this city. The final inspection and plugging, in order to ascertain the sound condition of each bale, can take place at any time subsequent, or at the time of shipment.

All certificates of inspection shall give the weight of each bale of Hay weighed and inspected. The expenses for inspection shall not exceed thirty (30) cents per ton of two thousand (2,000) pounds, and shall be divided equally between buyer and seller.

REGULATIONS FOR THE INSPECTION OF PROVISIONS.

REGULATION 1. For the examination of provisions sold as Standard, it shall be the duty of any Inspector properly appointed by the Association, on receiving notice, to go to any packing house or warehouse in the city, to examine provisions, in such quantities as may be required, selecting the same in such a manner, from the lots specified, as, in his judgment, will give a fair sample of the whole.

REG. 2. If, upon examination, the property is found, in all respects, up to the requirements of the classification of the grades adopted by the Association, he shall issue a certificate to that effect, which certificate shall state the number of packages, pieces or pounds examined, and also the number of packages, pieces or pounds in the lot to which the examination is intended to apply, and that the packages (if any) are in good merchantable order and condition. In the case of Lard, no certificate for inspection shall be issued unless every package is examined; but, on request of the owner or person ordering the inspection, the Inspector may examine a part of a lot, and issue a certificate of such examination, stating the number of packages examined, and also the whole number of packages in the lot.

REG. 3. When necessary to remove property for the convenience of examination, it shall be the duty of the Inspector to send for the same, that a fair sample may be obtained. In no case should a certificate be granted on samples delivered by the seller.

REG. 4. The fees for inspection shall be : For all Pickled Meats (including repacking and coopering), one dollar per package for first five packages. For Bulk or Boxed Meats, twenty-five cents per one thousand pounds. For Lard, five cents per package. For stripping Lard, one dollar per package. All inspection fees to be paid by the buyer unless the property is rejected; then to be paid by the seller.

REG. 5. It shall be the duty of the Inspector, when requested by the owner, either at any packing house, warehouse, or in yards provided by the Inspector, to overhaul and inspect provisions, according to the qualifications and classifications authorized; two hundred pounds of meat, with abundance of good salt, to be repacked into each barrel, and cooperage to be put in good order ; each barrel of Provisions that is sound, sweet and free from any and every defect, to have grade and date of inspection branded thereon, and the word "Repacked," as hereinafter specified; and any portion that is defective to be branded, in like manner, Rusty, Sour, or Tainted, as the case may be; the said brand to be placed with the Inspector's brand across the regular packer's brand ; such provisions, according to the grade or quality, to be classed as "Repacked 200 lbs."

REG. 6. The Inspectors shall use metallic letters and figures, marking iron or stencil for their dates and class of inspection.

REG. 7. It shall also be the duty of the Inspector to put his metallic brand, marking iron, or stencil on all samples of Provisions in tierces or barrels that he inspects; and he shall pass no Hog products in tierces or barrels as Standard, unless the real packer's name, location, number of pieces, date and weight of the products contained therein are branded according to these rules, on the head of every package.

REG. 8. Should the Inspector be called upon to inspect Pickled meats, and upon examination, he should be of the opinion that the number of pounds required by these rules had not been originally packed, he shall not pass them as Standard, but shall refer the matter at once to the Committee on Provision Inspection, who shall investigate, and if a satisfactory explanation can be given or arrived at, they shall instruct the Inspector to proceed and inspect and pass them; but if not satisfactory to the Committee, they shall, in their judgment, make the fact known to the Association in any way they may think most proper.

REG. 9. Contents of each package of Pickled Meats must show a reasonable uniformity in weight, according to its class.

REG. 10. It shall be the further duty of the Inspectors, during the packing season, to visit frequently the different packing houses to see that Provisions are properly dated and branded at time of being packed.

REG. 11. Dry Salted Rough Sides may be made into Short Rib or Short Clear Sides, and Dry Salted Short Rib Sides may be made into Short Clear Sides, if, in all other respects, they are up to the requirements, and shall be classed as Standard.

REG. 12. All the foregoing Regulations must be justly and liberally construed, and no property shall be rejected or condemned on mere technicalities.

REQUIREMENTS AS TO CUT AND PACKING OF HOG PRODUCTS.

BARRELED PORK.

MESS PORK.

Standard Mess Pork should be made from sides of well-fatted Hogs, split through or on one side of the backbone, and equal proportions on both sides, cut into strips of reasonably uniform width, properly flanked and not backstrapped.

One hundred and ninety (190) pounds of Green Meat, and between March 1 and November 1 two hundred (200) pounds, numbering not over sixteen (16) pieces, including the regular proportion of flank and shoulder cuts, placed four layers on edge, without excessive crowding or bruising, shall be packed in each barrel, with not less than thirty (30) pounds of coarse salt, and barrel filled with brine of full strength, or thirty (30) pounds of coarse salt, and in addition thereto, fifteen (15) pounds of salt, and barrel filled with cold water.

PRIME MESS PORK.

Prime Mess Pork should be made from the Shoulders and Sides of Hogs weighing from one hundred (100) to one hundred and seventy-five (175) pounds, net, to be cut as near as practicable into square pieces of four (4) pounds each; the shank of the Shoulder to be cut off close to the breast.

One hundred and ninety (190) pounds of Green Meat in the proportion of twenty (20) pieces of Shoulder cuts to thirty (30) pieces of Side cuts, shall be properly packed in each barrel, with not less than twenty (20) pounds of coarse salt, and barrel filled with brine of full strength; or, twenty (20) pounds of coarse salt, and in addition thereto, fifteen (15) pounds of salt, and barrel filled with water. There shall also be put into each barrel twelve (12) ounces of saltpetre.

EXTRA PRIME PORK.

Extra Prime Pork should be made from heavy untrimmed Shoulders, cut into three (3) pieces; the leg to be cut off close to the breast, and in all other respects to be cut, selected and packed as Mess Pork.

LIGHT MESS PORK.

Light Mess Pork should be made from Sides of reasonably well-fatted Hogs; and in all other respects to be cut, selected and packed same as Mess Pork, except that as many as twenty-two (22) pieces may be put into each barrel.

BACK PORK.

Back Pork should be made from backs of Hogs after bellies have been taken off, cut into pieces of about six (6) pounds each, and in all other respects to be cut, selected and packed in the same manner as Mess Pork.

EXTRA SHOULDER PORK.

Extra Shoulder Pork should be made from heavy trimmed Shoulders, cut into three (3) pieces; the leg to be cut off close to the breast, and in all other respects to be cut, selected and packed in the same manner as Mess Pork.

EXTRA CLEAR PORK.

Extra Clear Pork should be made from the Sides of extra heavy, well-fatted Hogs, the backbone and ribs to be taken out, the number of pieces in each barrel not to exceed fourteen (14), and in all other respects to be cut, selected and packed in the samer manner as Mess Pork.

CLEAR PORK.

Clear Pork should be made from the Sides of extra heavy, well-fatted Hogs, the backbone and half the rib next the backbone to be taken out, the number of pieces in each barrel not to exceed fourteen (14), and in all other respects to be cut, selected and packed in the same manner as Mess Pork.

CLEAR BACK PORK.

Clear Back Pork should be made from the backs of heavy, well-fatted

Hogs, after bellies have been taken off and backbone and ribs taken out, cut into pieces of about six (6) pounds each, and in all other respects to be packed in the same manner as Mess Pork.

RUMPS.

Rumps should be trimmed with only enough taken off to make them neat and smooth; the tails to be cut off close, and in all other respects to be cut, selected and packed in the same manner as Mess Pork.

PICKLED MEATS.

STANDARD SWEET PICKLED HAMS.

Standard Sweet Pickled Hams should be cut short and well rounded at the butt, properly faced, shank cut in or above the hock joint; to be reasonably uniform in size, and average, in lots, not to exceed sixteen (16) pounds. Three hundred (300) pounds, block weight, shall be packed in each tierce, with either twenty-four (24) pounds of salt, three (3) quarts of good syrup, twelve (12) ounces of saltpetre, and tierces filled with water; or tierce filled with sweet pickle, made according to above standard

STANDARD SWEET PICKLED SHOULDERS.

Standard Sweet Pickled Shoulders should be well cut and trimmed, reasonably uniform in size, and average, in lots, not to exceed sixteen (16) pounds. Three hundred (300) pounds, block weight, shall be packed in each tierce. Pickle the same as used for Hams.

NEW YORK SHOULDERS.

New York Shoulders should be made from small, smooth Hogs, shank cut off one inch above knee joint, trimmed close and smooth, reasonably uniform in size, and to average, in lots, not to exceed fourteen (14) pounds. Three hundred (300) pounds, block weight, shall be packed in each tierce. Pickle the same as used for Hams.

SWEET PICKLED BELLIES.

Sweet Pickled Bellies should be made from nice smooth Hogs, well cut and trimmed, to average, in lots, not to exceed fourteen (14) pounds

Three hundred (300) pounds, block weight, shall be packed in each tierce. Pickle the same as used for Hams.

BRANDING.

The packers' name, location, number of pieces, and date of packing, shall be branded on the head of each package of Pickled Meats at the time of packing.

UNIFORMITY OF PICKLED MEATS.

All Pickled Meats should be sized when packed—the light, medium and heavy separately, as nearly as practicable.

CUT MEATS.

HAMS.

Hams should be cut short, well rounded at the butt, properly faced, cut in or above the hock joint.

SHOULDERS.

Shoulders should be cut as close as possible to the back part of the forearm joint, butted off square on top; neckbone and short ribs taken out, blood vein lifted and cut out, breast flap to be trimmed off, and foot to be cut off in or above the knee joint.

BLADED SHOULDERS.

Bladed Shoulders should be cut the same as Standard Shoulders, excepting the shoulder-blade to be taken out and the corners rounded.

ROUGH SIDES.

Rough Sides should be made by splitting the Hog through or on one side of the backbone, and an equal proportion of both Sides must be delivered on sales to make them Standard.

SHORT CLEAR SIDES.

To make Short Clear Sides, the backbone and ribs should be taken out, henchbone and breastbone sawed or cut down smooth, and even with the face of the Side; feather of bladebone not to be taken out, and Sides not to be backstrapped or flanked.

SHORT RIB SIDES.

To make Short Rib Sides, the backbone should be taken out, henchbone and breastbone sawed or cut down smooth, and even with the face of the Side; feather of bladebone not to be taken out, and Sides not to be backstrapped or flanked.

LONG CLEAR SIDES.

To make Long Clear Sides, the backbone, shoulder bones and ribs must be taken out, leg cut off close to the brisket, henchbone and breastbone sawed or cut down smooth and even with the face of the Side, and Sides not to be backstrapped or flanked.

CUMBERLAND SIDES.

To make Cumberland Sides, the Side and Shoulder should be left together in one piece, leg cut off below the knee joint; shoulder ribs, neckbone and backbone taken out; blood vein lifted and cut out; henchbone and breastbone sawed or cut down smooth and even with the face of the Side, and Sides not to be backstrapped or flanked.

LONG RIB SIDES.

Long Rib Sides should be made same as Cumberlands, except that the shoulder bones must be taken out, and leg cut off close to the brisket.

STRETFORD SIDES.

Stretford Sides should be made from Hogs weighing about 140 to 160 pounds net; backbone and half of the ribs taken out, bladebone taken out, knuckle left in, and foot cut off close to the breast.

BIRMINGHAM SIDES.

Birmingham Sides should be made from Hogs weighing about 170 pounds net; backbone, ribs and bladebone taken out, pocket piece cut out and pocket nicely rounded, knucklebone left in, and leg cut off close to the breast.

SOUTH STAFFORDSHIRE SIDES.

South Staffordshire Sides should be made the same as Birmingham, except loin taken out full to top of shoulder blade, leaving only a thin strip of lean along the back; knuckle left in, and leg cut off close to the breast.

YORKSHIRE SIDES.

Yorkshire Sides should be made the same as Cumberlands, with ribs out and leg cut off about two inches above the knee.

IRISH CUT SIDES.

Irish Cut Sides should be made the same as Long Clear, except top of the pocket cut off, knuckle-bone left in.

LONG HAMS.

Long Hams should be cut from the Side by separating with a knife the hipbone from the rump, properly rounded out, foot unjointed at first joint below the hock joint.

SOUTH STAFFORDSHIRE HAMS.

South Staffordshire Hams should be cut short, hipbone taken out at socket joint, hock unjointed at first joint below the hock joint.

UNIFORMITY OF BOXED MEATS.

In packing Meats in boxes, the pieces should be classified—the light, medium and heavy separately, as nearly as practicable, in packages made to suit the different sizes.

LARD.

CHOICE LARD.

Choice Lard to be made from leaf and trimmings only, either steam or kettle rendered, the manner of rendering to be branded on each tierce.

PRIME STEAM LARD.

Prime Steam Lard shall be Standard made from the head, gut, leaf and trimmings, in the proportion in which the same came from the hog.

PACKAGES.

COOPERAGE.

Cooperage shall be made of well-seasoned White or Burr Oak, free from objectionable sap.

BARRELS.

For barrels, staves should be five eights ($\frac{5}{8}$) of an inch thick, twenty-nine (29) or thirty (30) inches long; heads eighteen (18) inches, one (1) inch thick in center, and three-eighths (⅜) at bevel; hoops hickory, or white oak, to be hooped not less that eleven-sixteenths (11-16).

TIERCES.

Tierces for Hams, Shoulders, Beef or Lard, should be thirty-two (32) inches long with a twenty-one (21) inch head, or thirty-three (33) inches long with a twenty and one-half (20½) inch head; staves to be chamfered at the head. Quality of staves and hoops to be the same as for barrels; staves (¾) of an inch thick; heads same thickness as for barrels; hooped eleven-sixteenth (11-16). Iron-bound tierces for Lard, Hams or Shoulders, shall be classed as Standard if made in compliance with the requirements of this rule, as to heading and staves, and hooped with not less than four good hoops on each end.

BOXES.

Boxes should be made of sound common boards, reasonably dry, one inch thick, dressed on one side, not over three strips to each end, side bottom or top; to have good, strong, hardwood, whitewood or sap pine stays inside each corner; should be well nailed and strapped with birch, oak or hickory straps around each end, to lap three inches on the cover. Boxes should be nailed together with tenpenny nails, and the stays nailed in with eightpenny nails.

THE UNION STOCK YARDS AND TRANSIT COMPANY

The supremacy that Chicago has attained as a business mart cannot be better illustrated than by a brief descriptive review of the Union Stock Yards and Transit Company. The advantages offered by this mammoth enterprise to Western dealers and feeders of live stock are unequaled in any market, either in the old or new world. The enterprise is owned by a chartered company with a paid-up capital. The amount of which we were unable to ascertain as the officers of the company declined to make it public, but there is no doubt that it runs into the millions.

This great bovine and porcine city consists of 345 acres—extending from Halsted street on the East to the Packing Houses on the West, running North to 47th street, thence South to the open prairies—and in its enterprising march, will have before a very long time hence, within its boundaries, all there ever was of the famous horsemen's sporting grounds, known as "Dexter Park." The yards are now said to be one mile in length by one-half mile in width, but are being extended in the direction mentioned.

They were opened for the reception of live stock on December 25th, 1865. As you enter from Halsted street, immediately on your left is the "Transit House," built at an expense of $250,000, which is furnished with exceeding neatness, and an air of comfort seems to pervade the entire premises. As you proceed along a wide avenue on a raised sidewalk until you have reached very nearly the center of the grounds, you come directly upon an unpretending looking one story brick building which is known as the Union Stock Yards National Bank, financially a formidable institution, and admirably managed by those having its interests in charge. When you have passed it, a plain looking two and one-half story brick building 60x380 feet is before you, this is called the "Ex-

change," and as you enter this building you are introduced to a very
large Exchange Hall on one side of which are located the Superintendent's, Secretary and Treasurer's offices with the telegraph office. On
the other side there is quite a stretch of an avenue, on either side of
which are located, both on this and the second floor, about 80 offices
which are occupied by the live stock commission merchants. These are
all surrounded with a saloon, restaurant, packers offices, offices for Eastern shippers, barber shop and fruit stand Upon ascending to the second
floor of this building, standing at almost any point there is presented to
the eye an animated scene—with countless herds of cattle and swine and
sheep enclosed in the pens—the whole grounds teeming with the bustle
and activity incident to buying, selling and transporting of stock. With
men hurrying hither and thither on horseback in the dispatch of varied
business matters and crowds of pedestrians apparently brimful of the
same purposes; then looking off to the West the city of packing houses,
some thirty in number, tower up in the distance and are easily discern-
ible; these together with the shrill whistle of the various incoming and
outgoing trains of cars loaded with live stock, make a grand and rare
sight indeed. There are some 40 miles of tracks connecting the yards
with all the railroads centering in Chicago. The arrangement for either
loading and unloading are as nearly perfect as is possible to conceive.
As is also the arrangement for the transfer of any number of cattle from
the cars of one railway to another. The pens for live stock vary in size
but are nearly all laid off square in shape, and are so constructed that
several can be thrown into one by merely opening gates, very similar to
the opening of doorways to the rooms of a house. Gates are also so arranged as to open across the roadway, enabling the turning of a drove
directly into a pen, and then closing after them. The cattle pens are
open, but those designed for hogs and sheep are covered. They are all
well fitted with troughs and hydrants, the latter connecting with the
water tanks which are kept supplied with pure water received from the
artesian wells that have been bored on the grounds. There are three
artesian wells situated in about the centre of the enclosure, one of which
is eleven hundred feet, and the other two, each twelve hundred feet
deep. There are over fifteen miles of macadamized streets running
through, and intersecting with each other in different parts of the Yards.
And forty miles of water and drainage pipes, forming a perfect net-work
running underneath, thoroughly accomplishing the desired result aimed
at.

The matter of weighing droves of cattle, sheep and hogs is an important one. The scales that are used throughout the Yards are the celebrated "Fairbanks." There are thirteen fifty-ton stock scales in constant use, besides numerous smaller ones needed for weighing hay, corn, etc. The company have been wise in making so judicious a selection in a matter so important to both the buyer and seller. The Fairbank's scales have been used from one end of the country to the other, and they have always at all places maintained their high character for perfect accuracy, and we believe are entitled to the supremacy they have attained as being superior to all others manufactured. They are regularly adjusted and every care is taken to provide for their perfect equilibrium. The weigh-masters are appointed by the officials of the Yards, and are not permitted to receive any fee or reward in any wise. The rules with which they must act in accordance, are rigid and exacting, to enforce a just performance of duty, and any well grounded complaint for non-performance of duty, as strictly laid down by the rules is an equivalent to a dismissal from further service. In convenient parts of the Yards are located a printing office from which is issued the "*Drover's Journal*," an ably conducted quarto newspaper, devoted exclusively to the interests of the live stock dealer and said to be the only newspaper of the kind published in the world; machine shops, the postoffice, depot buildings, and many other buildings used in the transaction of business pertaining to the receiving and shipping of live stock. From a critical examination it can be truthfully said, that on every hand, go whither you may over these vast grounds, there are evidences confronting you of great ability and wise forethought pervading the entire inclosure. It is apparent that the great enterprise is in the hands of men of master minds. Everything that is necessary which ingenious thought could suggest is provided; nothing seems to be forgotten, and from the improvements, that are being constantly made, any and every emergency that could possibly occur are being guarded against. This vast business enterprise has kept pace with the wonderful growth, arising from the constant settlements, occurring from year to year on the rich and bounteous lands of the Northwestern States by emigrants and others seeking permanent homes through tilling the soil and in raising of live stock. But it matters not where the locality may be, live stock is shipped from all points to these Yards, even as far distant as the feeding lands of Texas are, the shipments from thence are very large. Through its management, since its inception in the year 1865, to this date, the enterprise has proven a success. The business has been large and remunerative, but that the expenses which must necessarily accrue from the constant wear and tear of the yards, together with the general management of an organization of such immense magnitude cannot be otherwise than enormous in amount. To give some evidence of the outlay of money that is necessary from time to time to keep the grounds in good condition, we have only to refer to the proceedings which took place at the annual meeting of the Directors and Stockholders in the year 1875, when an appropriation was made for repairs and improvements, and the enlargement of the Yards, so as to meet the requirements of the constantly increasing live stock trade, for the large amount of about $300,000.

These improvements, necessary for the reconstruction and the repairing of the Yards were begun and completed under the supervision of John B. Sherman, E,sq., the able and indefatigable Superintendent, assisted by George T. Williams, Esq., the courteous and efficient Secretary of the company. Both of these gentlemen have been connected with this grand enterprise for many years past, and during all these years, the active agents ; and in a great measure, it is through their instrumentality, the Yards have been brought to their present prosperous condition. There are now one hundred and seventy-five acres of land under plank, and constructed as follows: One hundred acres of cattle yards, seventy-five acres of covered hog and sheep pens.

Twelve hundred cattle pens, sufficient to yard twenty thousand head of cattle, thirteen hundred hog pens, which provide for one hundred and fifty thousand hogs; three hundred sheep pens that will accommodate fifteen thousand sheep, and also stabling for fifteen hundred horses.

To give some conception of the magnitude of this business enterprise, we are enabled to state that the business transactions for the year ending December 31st, 1877, amounted to *ninety-nine million, twenty four thousand one hundred dollars*, and from the year 1872, to 1877, inclusive, *six hundred and twenty-one million, six hundred and fourteen thousand and three dollars*. These figures are colossal in amount, but they are nevertheless correct, and are living evidences of wonderful enterprise coupled with business sagacity.

In closing our remarks upon this vast business interest of our city, we extract the following from Griffith's Live Stock Annual," for the year ending 1877: "The past year has done much to strengthen the convictions which have existed in the minds of all practical men as to the suitableness of the situation which was chosen for the Great Central Live

Stock Market of the West, in its present stage of development. What the future may discover we are quite willing to leave to that future to determine. It may be that some few decades hence, stock yards as capacious as our own may be needed in that great growing territory of Wyoming, or in Nebraska, or Colorado, or Kansas; in either, or indeed in all, of these great growing centres of the live stock trade of the West, thriving, organized and capacious system of yards may be needed and built but for the present, we are in the best position conceivable to take charge of their stocks; and furnish them with prompt cash buyers for the same. We are sufficiently near to enable all those centres to transfer their herds to this market in a comparatively few hours, and in very nearly as good condition as when they leave their home pastures.

The entire Railroad interests of the East and West have made Chicago their objective point, where all the lines meet as in a focus, and from which they radiate to all the pasture lands of the West, and all the seaports, cities, towns, and villages of the East. May we not, therefor, without venturing within the line of the prophetic fairly state that such a center must, in the very nature of things continue for a lengthened period to occupy the high position we already have gained as the great and important live stock market of America."

The writer whom we have just quoted is quite warm in his expressions, but his enthusiasm has not betrayed him into making assertions that are other than really the facts. Here is located without any question of doubt the greatest live stock market in the world, and with the abundant facilities for reaching it, the unexampled inducements offered, must make the Union Stock Yard and Transit Company the objective point for a long time hence to the dealer and raiser of live stock of the West. The great and growing young States of Wyoming, Colorado, Kansas, and Nebraska must abide their time; it will come, but it is in the distant future yet. To be sure, each of these young States is being rapidly peopled with an abundance of brain and muscle that will eventually carry them to the front, and each will be a bright star in the constellation that form our proud union of States. But in their youth and as they are becoming stalwart and robust they must look to Chicago for assistance and support. And it is an agreeable reflection to the people of Chicago and those of the Northwest "to know that so vast an interest, a trust so important, is in the hands of a management of such acknowledged ability and trustworthiness."

UNION STOCK YARDS.

The money value of the live stock trade exceeds that of any other one product of America, but of the customs and laws peculiar to the business but little is known to those not directly connected therewith, we therefore give a somewhat detailed account of the mode of doing the work connected with the movement of stock to and in this city.

At the beginning of all live stock trade stands the farmer, who is sometimes the shipper of his own and his neighbor's beeves or hogs, but as a general rule this work is done by a class of men who were once called drovers but who are now shippers in name as in fact, since driving forms an important part of their duties. Some of these shippers have offices established in towns on the line of some railroad and there spend much of their time, buying the stock brought in by farmers, and making arrangements for the purchase and delivery of that which is perhaps not quite ready for sale. Others have no fixed office, but go about the district selecting and buying the animals on the farms, and agreeing upon the time and place of delivery. Arrived at the shipping point, the shipper, who has experience, assorts his stock, so far as may be convenient, shipping the best together, and the poorer by themselves. As a rule, regular shippers consign their stock to some house known to them, and go about getting together another consignment. Some send no one with their hogs to care for them, and where the distance to be traveled is not great, some send their cattle without any one to see that they go through in good condition. As a rule, however, the owner of the cattle or some one in his employ accompanies the consignment, to keep the cattle from lying down on the way. This is necessary, as in loading, the car is filled to its utmost capacity, that the animals may support each other and so ride more easily, and be less bruised by the motion of the train than they would be were there room for them to sway about. But some of the means taken to rouse to their feet such of the poor brutes as sink from exhaustion are scarcely so necessary, and are altogether barbarous, sharp spikes set in poles, savage hooks and other instruments of torture having been freely used until the efforts of the Humane Society put an end to the practice, or at least to the bringing of these instruments to the Stock Yards.

Arrived at the Yards, the stock is driven out upon a platform, which is even in height with the floors of the cars, and which extends with but few breaks around three sides of the Yards. From this platform an inclined plane leads to the paved ground. Down this the stock is driven, and from this moment the responsibility of the railroad company ends, and that of the Stock Yards company begins. At this "shute" the employes of the Union Stock Yards and Transit Company count, with the utmost care, the animals received from each car, noting the numbers of the car, the shute and the animals. Any shortage is at once noted in their numerous memorandum books, as is also the condition of the stock. The first count is considered as final in tracing losses. Beyond that one must go to the railroad company. The name of the consignor and that of the consignee, taken from the way-bills brought by the conductor of the train, are also entered in this—one of the most important—as it is the first entry made by the Stock Yards Company. The record appears thus

5 St. Louis, Oct. 30.

Consignor.	Consignee.		B.	P.	C.	H.	S.	Remarks.
John Brown.	Gregory, Cooley & Co.		10	13		175		4 Crips.
3131	3109	2559						7 Dead.
22	23	21						

To the initiated this reads: "Cars numbered 3131, 3109 and 2559 of the fifth train received in the St. Louis division on the thirtieth day of October, brought 175 hogs consigned by John Brown to Gregory, Cooley & Co. There were four crippled and seven dead hogs in these cars. The hogs from car number 3131 were unloaded into shute number 22, those from car 3109 into shute 23, and those in car 2559 into shute 21, and all were afterward put into pen number 13, in block 10. For any other kind of stock the entries would be essentially the same in form.

For greater convenience the yards are laid out into divisions popularly known as the Rock Island, the Burlington, the St. Louis, the Northwestern and the St. Paul, but officially they are described by the first

UNION STOCK YARDS NATIONAL BANK. (SEE PAGE 106.)

TEXAS CATTLE.

five letters of the alphabet. Above the corners of each block are signs upon which are plainly painted the letter of the division and the number of the block, while each pen has its number upon its gate. The pens for sheep and for hogs are roofed, and the whole yards are divided by streets and alleys, some of them paved and many of them planked, as are also most of the pens.

After the stock is driven to a pen and there locked in, the consignee gives on a printed card, furnished by the company, an order for the quantity of hay or of corn wanted for the stock, and it is allowed time to "get a good fill on." For the corn, one dollar per bushel is charged; for the hay, thirty dollars per ton, and for an abundant supply of pure water from the artesian wells, brought by pipes to troughs in each pen, nothing is charged. The custom is to give the stock time to eat all it will of the dry food, and then allow the water to flow into the troughs. As the stock has, as a usual thing, been for a long time deprived of food and water, it is not difficult to believe that the animals will fill themselves to the utmost. By this means a number of pounds of corn, costing the owner of the stock something less than two cents per pound, and water costing nothing, is sold for the current price for hogs, and hay costing a cent and a half per pound is sold for, it may be, the price of the best beeves. It is by considering this fact the stock owner is able to reconcile himself to the payment of prices which have led to much angry discussion, and to various legislative investigations, with, thus far, no change for the relief of the oppressed. It has been repeatedly shown that in the principal Western stock yards the charge made for the use of the many conveniences furnished are uniform. In the Kansas City, the St. Louis and Chicago Stock Yards, twenty-five cents each pays for yarding cattle, and eight cents each pays all yard charges on sheep and hogs. There is for feeding and watering no charge other than that included in the price for the corn or the hay. In some of the Eastern markets fifty cents per head is charged for yardage on cattle, and fifty dollars per ton for hay.

After the arrivals have filled themselves to the utmost they are ready for sale, unless the salesman decides to sort them before offering them to the buyers, many of whom purchase for some particular market or especial purpose, for which a certain description only of stock is suitable. The necessity for assorting is growing, especially in Chicago, where the greater part of the stock received is thus 'sorted. This assorting is an important matter in the hog trade, as through it a skillful sorter can make a great difference in favor of the buyer—if the salesman can be made to consent. Soon after the sale is made the stock is weighed, the date of the transaction, the number of the division and of the scale, the name of the buyer, the seller and the weighmaster, together with the number and weight of the animals being given upon a card furnished for the purpose by the company. After the price at which the stock was sold has been marked upon the back of the ticket it goes to the clerks in the office of the salesman, and by them is taken to the office of the Stock Yards Company, and when the buyer is financially responsible and has made suitable arrangements there, and a duplicate showing, substantially the same things, as appear upon the ticket, is given under the signature of the Secretary and the official stamp of the company. This duplicate is then taken by the clerk of the salesman to the office of the buyer to obtain his signature, after which it is deposited, like any check or draft, to the account of the party making the sale. If the buyer has not made an arrangement at the bank here for the payment of his duplicate, he pays in the office of the seller for the stock, and receives an order for its delivery to him. To buyers of known responsibility what is known as an "open order" is given by the commission man or broker, and upon the strength of this open order, stock consigned to the firm giving it can be taken without a written order from the yards, thus saving a vast amount of bother.

As soon as the duplicate is received, or the order given for the delivery of the stock, an account is rendered and the net proceeds start on the way to the consignor, except when directions from him have changed the usual course. Often the money for a consignment is in the hands of the owner before the commission man receives pay for the stock. Many shippers to this market use all their available means in buying a lot of stock, and to them the prompt remittance of the proceeds of a sale is most important. This the sharp competition between the commission houses here insures.

There are attending each consignment of stock back charges, payment of which is assumed by the Stock Yards Company. To these are added the bills for yardage, for hay or for corn. For these the stock is held, and will not be released until the account is paid, except when the house selling the stock has given bonds to the amount of ten thousand dollars to secure the company against losses. In each case the charges are allowed to accummulate until the end of the week, and the total is collected, usually on Monday.

Such is, briefly and very plainly stated, the usual course of business at the greatest live stock mart the world has ever known, but behind this are many peculiarities which would no doubt be interesting to the business public. Like other lines of trade this has its disagreeable features Losses are by no means infrequent, although in theory the commission business should be safe. Some shippers make an arrangement when they draw upon correspondents here, for what is supposed to be something less than the stock will sell for on this market. If the stock " pays out " the balance, if any, is sent to the shipper. If it does not "pay out" the balance is often left standing on the books of the salesman here until another consignment is lucky enough to cancel the account. Practically, the commission man who honors a draft buys stock he has not seen, upon the judgment of others, of whose ability and integrity he may or may not be sure. The Texas cattle trade has been especially burdened with this evil, for evil it is unmistakably. One cause of loss arises from the custom of receiving from buyers checks upon the city banks, although the purpose is to sell stock only for cash. In many instances these checks have come back endorsed "no funds," and sometimes under circumstances which left no room to doubt that the intention of the buyer was to defraud. Much has been said about refusing to accept any but certified checks or the currency for stock, but it is not likely that this will be done until live stock brokers shall have united for self-defence.

In view of the fact that the live stock trade is greater than any other single interest in America, it seems singular that those who do the business of selling for others have not organized for the purpose of remedying the evils attending the present method of doing the business. That such an organization could be made to overcome the evil no one seems to doubt, and why the matter does not command the attention of the commission merchants is a marvel.

RECEIPTS AND SALES OF LIVE STOCK.

To show the amount of business transacted at the yards, we take the following from the report for the year ending December 31, 1877, of George T. Williams, Esq., Secretary. The figures are large but less than those of each of the three years preceding. This deficiency in the receipts was mainly to be attributed to the inclement weather which prevailed during the closing months of the year, and which caused the roadways to be almost impassable:

Cattle received during the year	$ 1.033.151
Hogs received during the year	4,025.970
Sheep received during the year	310.240
Horses received during the year	7.874
Value of Cattle	44.425.500
Value of Hogs	54.337.600
Value of Sheep	1.473.600
Value of Horses	787.400
Total Valuation	$99.024.100

STOCK CAPACITY.—The yards will conveniently contain at one and the same time the following number of stock:

Cattle	20.000 Head
Hogs	150.000 Head
Sheep	15.000 Head
Horses	1.500 Head
Total Capacity	166.000 Head

The Live Stock Commission Merchants, Union Stock Yards.

Among the most notable features in the business machinery of the Union Stock Yards are the Live Stock Commission Merchants. There are about 70 different parties and firms at this time engaged in this line of business enterprise. That they are an absolute and indispensable necessity for the protection of the shipper of live stock there cannot be a doubt. Some of these firms have had a long and highly reputable experience in the business, having started with the opening of the Yards for the reception of live stock in the year 1865; and are now consequently familiar with all the various matters pertaining to this important business interest. Having an acquaintance with the numerous large purchasers for the Eastern markets, as well as those purchasing for export—as also the buyers for home consumption. It needs business firms of this stamp to do justice to the shipper; and the shipper of live stock should not entrust his business in the hands of others than this class. Some of these merchants did a most creditable thing years ago, when they were not as well posted in the business of the yards as they are now. Sales were then made frequently to irresponsible parties for considerable amounts. But let it be noted here to the credit of these merchants that they promptly rendered their accounts of sales accompanied with a check for each of the several amounts, thereby protecting the shipper and sustaining the losses themselves. This manly and honorable conduct on the part of these firms, who have in the past proven their trustworthiness we are pleased to learn has been appreciated by the dealers and shippers. As the business of the Yards is being concentrated and fast passing into the hands of those firms who have been most throroughly tried in years past and who have on all occasions promptly responded to all just demands made upon them.

Though every reliance can be placed on the correctness of the weighing to which we more particularly refer elsewhere, it should be remembered that this and all matters come under the vigilant eye of the commission merchants or their representatives from the moment the live stock is received in the Yards until it is sold. And everything is so minutely and systematically arranged that the shipper has no further trouble after he has arrived at the Yards and has passed his stock over to the hands of the merchant. The charges for the sale of live stock as a rule, are fifty cents per head for cattle, and six dollars a car load for hogs and sheep. The returns for the sale of stock are either handed over, or forwarded to the shippers the same day the stock is sold.

A. GREGORY.　　H. H. COOLEY.　　L. R. HASTING.　　E. D. DOTY.

GREGORY, COOLEY & CO.

—) COMMISSION DEALERS IN (—

LIVE STOCK,

Room 58 Exchange Building,

UNION STOCK YARDS,

CHICAGO, ILL.

Having been engaged in the Live Stock Commission business for the past twenty five years, we have grown up and been identified with the trade from its infancy, and having ample means, are enabled to make liberal advances on consignments, and make prompt payment for all sales made.

We also, have a branch office at Denison, Texas, for the handling of Texas Cattle.

REFERENCES:

Union Stock Yards National Bank, - - - -	U. S. Yards, CHICAGO
Corn Exchange National Bank, - - - - - - -	"
First National Bank, - - - - - - - -	"

THE PACKING HOUSES.

On the Western limits of the Union Stock Yards are located the Packing Houses, about thirty in number. They are huge in their dimensions, some of them measuring 400 by 400 feet, and spread over a vast area of ground, in fact the territory they occupy is sufficiently extensive to make a fair-sized city.

While it is generally known that Chicago is the principal meat packing point in the world, the idea exists in a vague form, and there are but comparatively few people who have a knowledge of the immensity of this branch of business enterprise. Hence the importance of presenting to our readers, facts and figures thereupon.

With this object in view we have taken the pains to obtain reliable information concerning this great industry, one of the chief elements of Chicago's remarkable growth and prosperity. To show the yearly progress of the packing business in Chicago we append a table of statistics giving the aggregate number of cattle and hogs packed in each year since 1853:

SEASON.	CATTLE.	HOGS.
1853	24,663	44,156
1854	25,431	52,849
1855	23,691	73,694
1856	28,972	80,380
1857	14,971	74,000
1858	34,675	99,262
1859	45,503	179,685
1860	51,606	151,339
1861	34,624	271,805
1862	53,703	505,691
1863	39,687	970,264
1864	70,086	904,059
1865	92,459	760,514
1866	27,172	507,355
1867	25,994	649,332
1868	35,548	706,226
1869	26,950	597,954
1870	31,963	688,140
1871	21,254	919,197
1872	16,080	1,225,296
1873	15,755	1,456,650
1874	21,712	1,826,560
1875	41,192	2,136,716
1876	68,788	2,380,846
1877	92,574	3,079,749

The provision trade of this city has grown more rapidly within the past ten or twelve years than any other, and Chicago is now conceded by all to be the centre, and to a large extent the regulator of this vast business interest. The area of territory from which live stock is drawn to this market is constantly extending, the newly-settled States and territories contributing largely to swell the volume of our receipts.

The packing of hogs has quadrupled within the time specified, as has also the quantity of meats sent to this market for sale. The business gives employment to immense lines of capital and to thousands of persons, from the highest order of commercial talent to the lowest class of laborers, and from present indications promises to be one of constant growth; in the near future far surpassing its present grand proportions. The trade in provisions, besides being largely for consumptive demand, has also become one of a speculative character, the latter class of operations being largely confined to mess pork and lard. The magnitude of transactions in these articles, is to conservative merchants of the old style decidedly startling, but these are conducted with less of friction, and probably with more generally satisfactory results, than similar operations in grain. The business of some of these packing and provision companies is so stupendous as to be almost incredible. And yet we are only stating facts. In the busy season, their daily payments for hogs and cattle amount to from $50,000 to $150,000. And during four or five consecutive months they will have slaughtered on an average 7,500 to 8,000 hogs a day. The wonder is where they all find a market for consumption, but it should be remembered, their field is the world. Besides a heavy and increasing export trade to all the markets of Europe, the shipments to the South, West to California, and East to New York and New England are constant and very large.

The business of packing is now carried on both during the summer and winter. The summer packing is comparatively a new feature of the trade, but it is now pursued with entire success. Experience having satisfied packers that pork put down in summer is quite as good and possesses equal keeping properties to that packed in winter, and that there is no more danger, if proper care be exercised of the product souring or deteriorating in quality in summer than in winter. Hence the business of summer packing is now regarded as a fixture, as the summer packed meats have grown in favor, both in this country and Europe. So that there is not now, as heretofore, a long vacation observed, lasting from March to October.

The progress that Chicago is making in this branch of industry and trade, is unprecedented. For twenty-five years, with slight variations, there has been a steady and increasing growth. It is well known at this time, that for the season, as it is termed, for 1878, the packing of hogs will approximate about *four million five hundred thousand.* This is a large increase over the preceding season for 1877. It is however confidently predicted by those engaged in the business, that the time is not far distant in the future, when the packing of hogs in this city will have reached the extraordinary figure of *ten million*, during what is regarded as the packing season or seasons for the year. But as regard the volume of business in this particular business enterprise, Chicago stands to-day without a rival. She has so completely overshadowed all other points, that they can not be mentioned as competitors.

TRANSIT HOUSE.

UNION STOCK YARDS.

The " Transit House " located at the Union Stock Yards, built expressly for the accommodation of Stock dealers. Is a massive, and quite pretentious fivestory and attic brick structure—with cupola, which is surrounded by a veranda, from which the guests of the House can have a magnificent view of the yards, together with a panoramic sight of the city of Chicago, and the Lake. It is furnished neatly and comfortably throughout, and some of the rooms have the convenience of hot and cold baths. The table at all times is excellent, and the meats are of that superior order, that the most critical epicure can have his sensitive taste satisfied here.

The charges for the accommodation afforded are very moderate, ranging from $1.50 to $2.00 per day, and from $6 to $14 per week. Meals 50 cents each. There are both steam and horse car conveniences running to and from the city, giving to the guests every opportunity to visit places of amusement during the evening. Telegraphic reports of stock to arrive, are received daily.

THE UNION STOCK YARDS NATIONAL BANK.

The Union Stock Yard's National Bank is an unpretending one-story building, which adjoins the "Exchange." It is, however, an important and effective auxilliary in facilitating the general business of the Yards; and the amount of business transacted here is simply enormous, reaching as high as one hundred and twenty million dollars annually. Such an institution was an absolute necessity and had therefore to be provided. Since its establishment, the enterprise has proven a grand success, and is receiving the support of all the prominent live stock dealers in the West. The institution has been admirably managed by its former cashier, E. S. Stickney, Esq., but who has since the decease of the former President, Mancell Talcott, Esq., succeeded to the Presidency, Mr. Stickney has proven himself to be an able financier, and it may be said that it has been mostly through his instrumentality that the Bank has secured the favor and confidence of the Banking interests of the entire country. Whilst Mr. Stickney has with marked ability managed the executive duties pertaining to his official position, it is but proper to say, he has behind him a board of directors, who are as able and discriminating in judgment on financial affairs as any other set of men in the country. And it is through such management of its affairs that the Bank has so justly earned its high character for being one of the soundest and best managed financial institutions in the country.

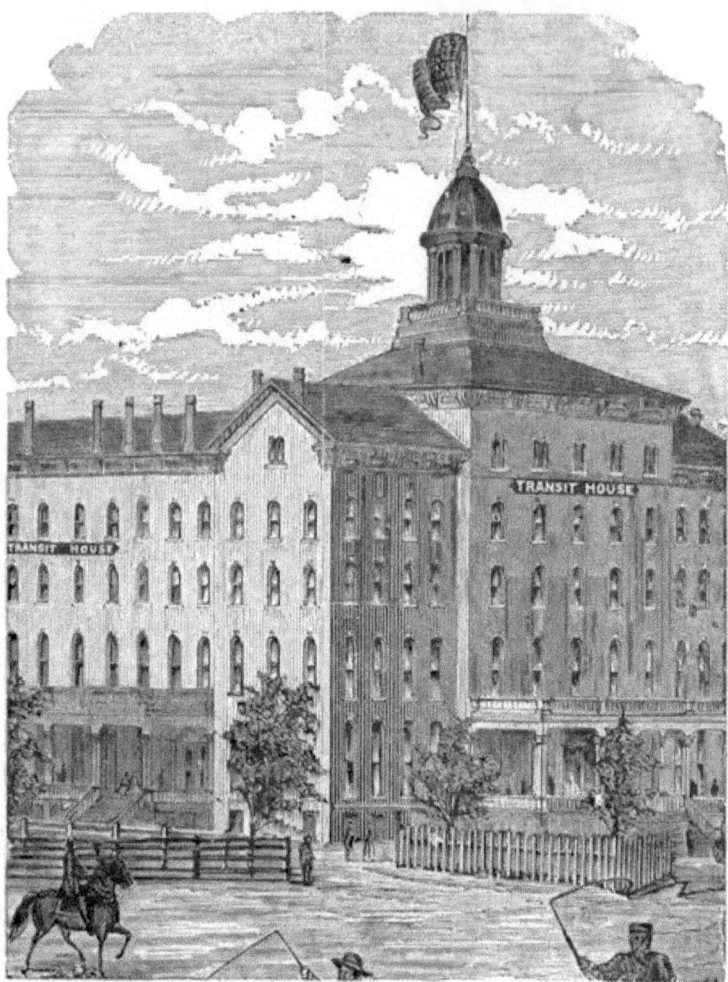

TRANSIT HOUSE.

Lumberman's Exchange of Chicago.

(Chartered by the State of Illinois, April 2d, 1869.)

Officers and Committees for the year ending the first Monday in March, 1879.

OFFICERS.

THADDEUS DEAN,	*President.*
JOHN McLAREN,	*Vice President.*
GEO. E. STOCKBRIDGE,	*Secretary.*
A. G. VAN SCHAICK,	*Treasurer.*

DIRECTORS.

THADDEUS DEAN.	HORACE W. CHASE.	ROBERT L. HENRY.
MALCOLM McDONALD.	A. P. KELLEY.	S. K. MARTIN.
A. G. VAN SCHAICK.	ALEXANDER OFFICER.	S. A. IRISH.
B. F. FERGUSON.	I. K. HAMILTON.	C. C. THOMPSON.
	JOHN McLAREN.	

COMMITTEE OF ARBITRATION.

J. B. Thompson.	J. H. Skeele.	Jas. H. Swan.
	Jas. McMullen.	M. B. Hull.

COMMITTEE OF APPEALS.

Jas. C. Brooks.	T. W. Harvey.	Geo. E. Wood.
	E. K. Hubbard.	Wayne B. Chatfield.

EXECUTIVE AND AUDIT COMMITTEE.

Jno. McLaren.	S. A. Irish.	I. K. Hamilton.

COMMITTEE OF INSPECTION.

Malcolm McDonald.	S. A. Irish.	Alex. Officer.
	B. F. Ferguson.	S. K. Martin.

COMMITTEE ON DOCKS.

Jno. McLaren.	S. A. Irish.	A. G. Van Schaick.

The Past and Present Executive Officers of the Lumberman's Exchange.

T. M. Avery, the first president of the Lumberman's Exchange, was elected to the chair in 1869 for the year ending the first Monday in March, 1870, and has been succeeded in each of the subsequent years since that date by—

Artemas Carter	during	1870 and	1871,
W. D. Houghtaling	"	1871 "	1873,
A. G. Van Schaick	"	1873 "	1874,
William Blanchard	"	1874 "	1875,
A. C. Calkins	"	1875 "	1876,
Thaddeus Dean	"	1876 "	1877,
Malcolm McDonald	"	1877 "	1878,
Thaddeus Dean	"	1878 "	1879.

W. L. Southworth was the first Secretary, and continued to occupy that position from 1869 to 1874, at which date he was succeeded by George E. Stockbridge, who still performs its official duties.

All of the gentlemen who have occupied the Chair are still living, and largely engaged in the lumber trade, with the exception of Artemas Carter, who died honored and respected by all who knew him on May 10th, 1877.

Receipts and Shipments of Lumber,

From 1847 to 1877, inclusive.

YEAR.	RECEIPTS.		SHIPMENTS.	
	Lumber, feet	Shingles, No.	Lumber, feet	Shingles, No
1847	32,118,225	12,148,500	....	....
1848	60,009,250	20,050,000	....	....
1849	73,259,553	39,057,750	....	....
1850	100,364,779	55,423,750	....	....
1851	125,056,437	60,338,250	....	....
1852	147,816,232	77,080,500	70,740,271	55,851,038
1853	202,101,078	93,483,784	88,909,348	71,442,550
1854	228,336,783	82,061,250	133,131,872	92,506,301
1855	306,547,401	108,647,250	215,585,254	134,793,250
1856	456,673,169	135,876,000	243,387,732	115,563,250
1857	459,639,198	131,830,250	311,608,793	154,827,750
1858	278,943,000	127,565,000	242,793,268	150,129,250
1859	302,845,207	165,927,000	226,120,389	195,117,700
1860	262,494,626	127,894,000	225,372,340	168,302,525
1861	249,308,705	79,356,000	189,379,445	94,421,186
1862	305,674,045	131,255,000	189,277,079	55,761,630
1863	413,301,818	172,364,875	221,709,330	102,634,447
1864	501,592,406	190,169,750	269,496,579	138,447,256
1865	647,145,734	310,897,350	385,353,678	258,351,450
1866	730,057,168	400,125,250	422,313,266	422,339,715
1867	882,661,770	447,039,275	518,978,354	480,930,500
1868	1,028,494,789	514,434,100	551,989,806	537,497,074
1869	997,736,942	673,166,000	581,533,480	638,317,840
1870	1,018,998,685	652,091,000	583,490,634	666,247,775
1871	1,039,328,375	647,595,000	541,222,543	558,385,350
1872	1,183,659,280	610,824,420	417,827,375	436,827,375
1873	1,123,368,671	517,923,000	561,544,379	407,505,650
1874	1,053,952,155	605,338,000	....	....
1875	1,157,194,432	635,708,000	....	....
1876	1,039,785,266	566,978,000	....	....
1877	1,066,462,361	546,442,000	586,722,821	170,410,785

LUMBER STATISTICS.

The receipts of Lumber in 1877 have been 1,066,452,361 feet, and the shipments 586,722,821 feet. The receipts of Shingles for the year have been 546,409,000, and the shipments 170,410,785.

The stocks on hand in the city at the begining of each of the last four years were as follows:

ARTICLES.		Jan. 1, 1878.	Jan. 1, 1877.	Jan. 1, 1876.	Jan. 1, 1875.
Sawed Pine Lumber and Timber......	Feet.	385,560,024	392,380,182	352,578,336	344,309,373
Hewn Pine Timber....................	Feet.	....	825	9,391	142,902
Shingles............................	Number.	125,040,000	97,467,000	83,230,750	81,019,990
Lath...............................	Pieces.	43,694,800	36,823,400	47,058,350	39,551,850
Pickets............................	Pieces.	2,296,020	3,386,617	2,380,928	2,489,981
Cedar Posts............	Number.	380,341	442,319	416,636	290,583

Average Weekly Prices of Lumber, Shingles and Lath, Vessel Cargo, during the Season of Navigation for the year 1877.

COMPILED BY GEO. E. STOCKBRIDGE, ESQ., SECRETARY OF THE LUMBERMAN'S EXCHANGE.

WEEK ENDING		Choice Mill Run Lumber, per M feet.	Medium Mill Run Lumber, per M feet.	Coarse Common Lumber, per M feet.	Ordinary Joists and Scantling, per M feet.	A Sawed Shingles, per M.	Lath per M
April.....................	14	$12 00	... ..	$9 25	.....	$2 05	....
....	21	12 00	..	9 00	$7 50	2 05	.....
....	28	12 00	$10 25	9 00	7 25	2 00	. ....
May......................	5	12 00	10 25	9 00	7 00	2 00	. ...
....	12	12 25	10 25	9 00	7 00	2 00	....
....	19	12 25	10 50	9 00	7 00	2 00	.....
....	26	12 25	10 50	9 00	7 25	2 00	$1 20
June	2	12 50	10 50	9 00	7 50	2 00	1 25
....	9	12 00	11 00	9 00	8 00	2 00	1 25
....	16	12 00	11 50	9 00	7 75	2 00	1 25
....	23	12 50	10 75	9 50	7 25	2 00	1 25
....	30	12 50	11 00	9 25	7 00	2 00	1 25
July......................	7	12 00	11 00	9 00	7 25	2 00	1 25
....	14	12 00	10 05	9 00	7 37½	1 90	1 25
....	21	12 00	10 50	9 25	7 37½	1 90	1 25
....	28	12 00	10 00	8 50	7 25	1 85	1 20
August...................	4	11 75	10 25	8 50	7 50	1 85	1 20
....	11	11 75	10 12½	8 50	7 60	1 85	1 20
....	18	12 25	11 00	8 50	7 50	1 85	1 20
....	26	12 50	11 00	8 50	7 50	1 85	1 20
September................	1	13 00	10 75	8 50	7 50	1 90	1 25
....	8	13 00	11 25	9 00	7 00	1 90	1 25
....	15	13 00	11 50	9 50	7 25	1 95	1 25
....	22	13 50	11 50	9 50	7 50	2 00	1 25
....	29	14 10	11 50	9 00	7 50	2 00	1 25
October..................	6	14 00	11 50	9 00	8 00	2 00	1 25
....	13	14 00	12 00	9 50	8 25	2 12½	1 25
....	20	14 00	12 00	9 50	8 75	2 25	1 25
....	27	14 12	12 00	9 50	8 75	2 25	1 25
November.................	3	14 00½	12 50	9 50	8 00	2 25	1 25
....	10	14 50	12 25	9 50	7 50	2 25	1 25
....	17	15 50	12 00	9 50	7 75	2 25	1 40
....	24	15 50	12 00	9 50	7 75	2 25	1 50
December	1	15 00	11 50	9 50	7 75	2 25	1 60
....	8		11 00	9 50	7 50	2 25	1 60

Lumberman's Exchange,

And the Lumber Trade of Chicago.

Keeping pace with all other commercial interests of the city until the business attained prodigious proportions, the lumbermen of Chicago found it a necessity to organize, in the year 1869, "The Lumberman's Exchange," and gave the reasons therefor in the preamble to the rules and by-laws governing the association, which are herewith given. "Chicago having become the great lumber market of the Northwest, situated midway between the pineries of the lakes and the sections that are destitute of lumber, enjoying unsurpassed facilities of transportation, both by lake and railway; with this vast business employing an amount of capital second to no other branch of trade we deem it important that an organization should be effected which should embrace this entire lumber interest, and further believing that this organization is demanded, to regulate transactions, adjust differences, promote fair dealing, and furnish all possible information that can benefit its members, we hereby organize an association."

The necessities for such an association were abundant, and the success that has attended it since its organization have proven the wisdom of its formation. The city of Chicago is most admirably situated for a lumber market. The lumber regions of Michigan and Wisconsin, inexhaustible as it would almost seem, are all accessible to the lakes, and lumber can be transported hither at a trifling expense, so that in purchasing here, dealers in remote places can do almost as well as if they were to transact their business in the very heart of the lumber region, which is many miles distant. This very fact coupled with another, that her merchants having an almost new and extensive part of our country (the Northwestern States), and which is in a very great measure barren of timber to supply with lumber, have made her what she is to-day, the

greatest lumber market of the world. For many years Albany, N. Y., enjoyed this distinction, and is quite an important market yet, but sinks into insignificance when compared with the metropolis of the West.

There are in the confines of Chicago at this time over two hundred establishments engaged in the business as dealers, manufacturers, commission men, and planing mill operators, and the subordinates connected therewith if collected together in a body, would form a fair sized army for invasion, and in the prosecution of this vast business there is employed an estimated capital of eighty million dollars both in Chicago and at the mills in the lumber country.

The growth of the business from its comparative insignificance in the year 1847, which is shown by a tabulated statement further on, to its present extraordinary dimensions seem marvelous. But we might ask, what is either wonderful or marvelous in a city that has made such gigantic and unparalleled strides in commerce in so short a period of time as Chicago has done? Her statistics in each department of trade are before the world, and we leave it to such evidence, to bear testimony to the position she is entitled to.

The membership of the " Lumberman's Exchange " is composed of nearly all of the leading lumber firms of the city, who contribute liberally to its support. It furnishes to the trade figures of the stock on hand on the first of each month, and keeps it informed of the stock of lumber and logs at competing points. Its management throughout the administrations of its different executive officers since its organization has been of so high an order that it is regarded by the trade as the model Lumber Exchange of the country, and its statistics are considered valuable information to form the basis of individual opinion at all times.

The lumbermen of Chicago are a wide-awake, active and intelligent body of men, and some of them rank among the foremost business men of the Northwest. And it is such men that have materially contributed to give to Chicago her wide-spread fame for peerless enterprise, indomitable perseverance and energy, business sagacity and commercial integrity.

Lumber Inspection.

NOTE.—We are indebted to Geo. E. Stockbridge, Esq., the efficient and esteemed secretary of the Lumberman's Exchange for the following information, and we herewith avail ourselves of the occasion to make our acknowledgments for this and other courtesies.

There are in practice in the Chicago lumber market, three inspections, viz: Yard inspection, or when the seller of a cargo of lumber agrees to sell by the sorting of the yard to whom the lumber is sold, and the old Chicago Lumberman's Board of Trade of inspection, which is however very rarely used, and the following inspection: When a cargo is sold by inspection, and no inspection stated, is the legal inspection of the Lumberman's Exchange and the trade generally, but ninety-five per cent. of all the lumber sold by cargo is sold straight measure, or as the cargo runs without inspection.

On March 15th, 1875, the following resolutions were adopted unanimously at a meeting of the members of the Lumberman's Exchange, and still continue to have legal force under this date:

Resolved, That the rules governing the grades and qualities of lumber as inspected from cargoes in the city of Chicago at present in force, be and the same are hereby repealed.

Resolved, That we, the Directors of the Lumberman's Exchange of Chicago do hereby adopt the following as the standard for the inspection of lumber in this market, viz:

All the merchantable white pine lumber shall be classified as follows for the purpose of inspection. First clear, second clear, third clear, common, and culls, and boards six inches wide, shall be known as strips; Norway pine shall be classified as common and culls, except as hereinafter provided.

First clear lumber shall not be less than eight inches wide, twelve feet long and one inch thick, and at such width and up to ten inches wide, shall be free from all imperfections. If the width is twelve inches, defects shall be allowed that will be equal in injury to the knot of one inch in diameter, or sap that will be equal to one and one-half inches on one surface. If the width is sixteen, defects shall be allowed that will be equal in injury to a knot of two inches in diameter, or sap that will be equal to two inches on one surface. If the width is twenty inches.

in diameter, or sap that will be equal to four inches in width on the edges. If the width is twenty inches, defects shall be allowed that shall be equal in injury to a knot of three inches in diameter, or sap that will be equal to five inches in width on the edges. A straight split shall be allowed in this quality as before, provided in boards of the width of twelve inches and over, and counted as one defect.

Third clear lumber shall not be less than seven inches wide, twelve feet long and one inch thick, and at such width and up to ten inches, defects shall be allowed that will be equal in injury to a knot one and a half inches in diameter, or sap that will be equal to one and a half inches in width on the best side. If the width is twelve inches, defects shall be allowed that will be equal in injury to a knot of two and a half inches in diameter, or sap that will be equal to two inches wide on the best side. If the width is sixteen inches, defects shall be allowed that will be equal in injury to a knot of four inches in diameter, or sap that will be equal to four inches wide on the best side. If the width is twenty inches, defects shall be allowed that will be equal to injury to a knot of five inches in diameter, or sap that will be equal to six inches on the best side. But sap in no case to exceed one-half the surface on the poorest side. In this quality shall be included pieces ten feet long, and not to have more than a due proportion of defects. Also, all pieces six inches wide and more than one inch thick, with not more than two small sound knots, or sap more than one inch in width on one side.

First clear strips shall be six inches wide, one inch thick, and not less than twelve feet in length and free from all inspections.

Second clear strips shall be the length, width and thickness of first clear, and may have two small sound knots, or if no knots, sap equal to one inch in width on one edge of one side.

Third clear strips shall be of the width and thickness of first clear strips, and may have three small sound knots with sap one inch on one side, but if no knots, then sap equal to two inches on one side may be allowed to be free from rot, split and shake. First and second clear Norway strips of full width and thickness, and first and second clear white pine strips, ten feet in length, also first and second clear strips rejected on account of thickness and not less than five inches in width shall be classed in this quality.

Common lumber shall include all boards, planks, scantlings, strips, joist, timber and lumber not otherwise defined, which is not as good as third clear, but is generally of a sound character, well manufactured, of defects shall be allowed that will be equal in injury to a knot two and one-half inches in diameter, or sap that will be equal to three inches in width on one surface.

The Inspector shall take particular notice, and shall allow a due proportion of defects, for all pieces of widths between or above the given standard; also shall allow additional defects as the lengths increase above twelve feet long in proportion to such increased dimensions. He shall also allow as follows, in each of the three grades of clear lumber, viz: For each additional half inch in thickness, additional defects in proportion, that shall be equal in injury to a knot of one quarter of an inch more in diameter, or sap that will be equal to one-quarter of an inch more in width. All the pieces shall be well manufactured and of full thickness, and all sap to be free from black stain, that is of such character that cannot be removed by dressing, and no piece shall be allowed with more than one straight split, and that not to be over one-fifth the length of the piece, which shall be counted as one defect.

Second clear lumber shall *not* be less than eight inches wide, twelve feet long and one inch thick, and at such width and up to ten inches wide, defects shall be allowed that will be equal in injury to a knot of three quarters of an inch in diameter, or sap that will be equal to three-quarters of an inch in width on one surface. If the width is twelve inches, defects shall be allowed that will equal in injury to a knot one and one-half inches in diameter, or sap that will be equal to three inches in width on the edges. If the width is sixteen inches, defects shall be full thickness, and free from large loose knots, and bad shakes that show on both sides of the pieces. Scantlings, joists and timber must be free from imperfections which so weaken the piece that it cannot be used for substantial building purposes. Scantling, joist and timber made from worm-eaten logs, and pieces with a small streak of rot, when not so badly damaged as to render the same unfit for ordinary uses of common lumber, shall belong to this quality. One straight split shall be allowed, provided that it does not exceed one quarter the length of the piece. Pieces that have not more than two auger holes which are placed near shall be allowed in this quality, provided they are measured in length of even numbers between said augur holes, and conform in all other respects to the requirements of this quality. No lumber under ten feet in length shall be considered as merchantable.

Culls shall constitute the lowest grade of merchantable lumber, and shall include all lumber not as good as common, which can be used for ordinary purposes without a waste of more than one-half.

The meeting then adjourned, to meet at the rooms of the Lumberman's Board of Trade on Tuesday, March 16, 1879.

GOSS & PHILLIPS MANUFACTURING COMPANY.

LUMBER, SASH, DOORS, BLINDS, ETC.

The chronicler of Chicago's progress meets with illustrations numerous and vivid as he visits the almost innumerable prominent houses to be found in the city. Some of these establishments have a history of their own, running back many years. Others are just making a history, and as we first visit one and then another we find ample food for reflection in the form of memoranda relative to the proportions and progress of our vast manufacturing industries. In the changes that have accompanied the flight of time, many of the old firms of to-day have been colaborers in the laudable work of building up and extending the commercial interests of our city, and by their enterprising efforts the numerous productive industries that have made the "Garden City" famous throughout this country and Europe have flourished to a degree surprising to the manufacturers of other and less fortunate cities.

It is well known, as we have stated, that Chicago is the leading lumber market of the world, and by reason of her unequaled geographical position as a distributing point, and the superior class of products turned out by her manufacturers, she has gained a prestige second to that of no other commercial centre in either hemisphere.

Among all the establishments engaged in the lumber business and manufacture in Chicago, there is none more widely known or in higher repute than the

GOSS & PHILLIPS MANUFACTURING COMPANY.

This is the oldest concern in this business in the city, having been started in 1848 by Mr. Daniel Goss, the present Vice President of the Company. The trade assumed extensive proportions within a few years thereafter, and in 1871 a stock company was organized, since which time the business has attained a magnitude excelled by no similar establishment in the country. The present officers of the company are: William B. Phillips, President; Daniel Goss, Vice President; Cornelius Curtis, Secretary and Treasurer.

In the production of sash, doors, blinds, moldings, balusters, newels, stair rails, etc., they transact an immense and constantly increasing business, having unsurpassed facilities therfor. In the department of balus-

ters, newels and stair rails they do the handsomest and most elaborate work of any concern in the Union. Some elegant and notable specimens of their taste and skill in this line may be seen in the Palmer House and the Grand Pacific Hotel, Chicago, the Fisk University, Nashville, Tenn., the residence of the British Minister at Washington, D. C., and the Peoria Court House as well as in many other of the finest public and private buildings throughout the country.

An important auxiliary of their business is the manufacture of all kinds of materials for dwellings, etc., which can be transported to any part of the world and erected without any difficulty, every piece being accurately fitted, marked and numbered. Their trade in all lines extends not only to all sections of the United States, but to South America, Australia, Southern Africa and other foreign countries.

A new feature of their business is the manufacture of the Behel patent blind, which is generally conceded to be the best and most desirable blind extant. It is adapted for both outside and inside use, and effectually excludes rain, dust and sunlight. Its cost is but slightly in excess of the ordinary blinds, and it is being very extensively adopted by builders here and elsewhere, giving entire satisfaction in every case. They will furnish to applicants an illustrated circular containing full information. They also issue descriptive catalogues of all their manufactures.

Some idea of the magnitude of their business may be formed from the fact that they consume in their productions the enormous amount of 13,000,000 feet of lumber annually. Their works, located on West Twenty-second and Fisk streets, are the most extensive of the kind in the country, are substantially constructed of brick, and contain the latest improved machinery and appliances for the prosecution of their varied industries. From 300 to 350 experienced workmen are now employed, and every department is operated to its full capacity in order to promptly meet the requirements of their trade. Their docks, buildings and yards cover a large area, affording conveniences and facilities for all operations. In addition to their manufacturing, they assort, dock, dress and ship largely of lumber of every grade and kind. All regular sizes and styles of their products are kept constantly in stock, so that orders for either the home or export trade can be promptly supplied.

PRODUCE EXCHANGE.

PRESIDENT........................ ....D. RICHARDS.
FIRST VICE-PRESIDENT............W. W. DEXTER.
SECOND VICE-PRESIDENT.............CHAS. BALTZ.
SECRETARY AND TREASURER.....JOHN E. COWLES.

COMMITTEE OF ARBITRATION.

C. H. WEAVER,   F. NICKERSON,
J. M. CYRUS,   NATHAN SMITH,
A. BUTTS,   A. L. TUCKER,
J. N. ADAMS,   C. C. RICE.

DIRECTORS.

GEORGE P. BRAUN,   A. L. TUCKER.
B. F. BAKER.   C. F. DEXTER.
             A. ALBRO.

COMMITTEE OF APPEALS.

A. L. BARBER,   N. W. HEWES,
P. B. WEARE,   HENRY HEMMELGARN,
L. S. CHASE,   L. E. FITTS,
E. S. WATTS,   JOHN P. BARRON.

The Produce Exchange and the Produce Commission Business

OF CHICAGO.

The Produce Commission Merchants of Chicago, believing that, as an independent body of the Board of Trade, it would be mutually advantageous to the producer and the buyer to establish a Produce Exchange " to foster and protect the interests which are not represented by the Board of Trade, as well as to gain the advantages resulting from the centralization of interests by bringing the buyer and seller at once together; thus giving to the buyer a place where he can at all times find property for sale, and the seller a mart for his merchandise," permanently organized on May 9, 1874, by the adoption of a Constitution and By-Laws and the election of officers, the " Produce Exchange of Chicago."

The advantages and objects in view to be gained in the formation of such an association, having under its control the equitable interests of both buyer and seller, and the providing to each party a suitable business resort, were, in every manner commendable, and imparted to the enterprise an impress of stability and dignity that properly belong to a body of high-minded, honorable business men. And when we consider the steady and rapid growth of the West—its marvelous progress in commerce, the immensity of its productions, its ability, when commensurately peopled with producers, as it most assuredly will be to supply the wants and feed the hungry millions of the world—the vast amount of business controlled at this time by the commission merchants, it was imperative to meet the demands arising therefrom that such an association should be organized, and we are pleased to state that since its formation it has fully responded to all the purposes for which it was established.

The Chicago market offers great and unsurpassed inducements to the shippers of produce of the West, possessing a net-work of railway lines radiating to and intersecting at all points in every direction, together with a water route of limitless capacity which she derives from Lake Michigan and the canal system to receive merchandise. She has likewise equal facilities for its shipment to each and all of the Eastern and Southern markets, and her merchants, with keen foresight and full appreciation of the situation to protect the interest of the shippers have made abundant provisions of improved facilities in the storing of all articles of produce. Cool and dry storage has been provided to an extent which can not be found in any other city of the country. And acting in concert with the prevailing spirit of enterprise, everything has been done that will make this market acceptable and advantageous both to the producer and the buyer. And we think it is not arrogant or undemonstrable for Chicago to claim that she is the Metropolis of the West. For the statistics of the amount of business transacted annually in all departments of commercial pursuits, when compared with those of other cities, establish the fact that she is pre-eminently the center of trade of the West. And with the knowledge that the great and rapidly growing States of the North West are emptying their varied productions into her lap, induces the buyers from all parts of the country to make this market their objective point for their operations. In the very nature of things Chicago is destined ever to be the great depot and distributing point for the agricultural products of the West—and her hundreds of enterprising and reliable commission merchants are determined to keep abreast of the requirements of this constantly expanding traffic.

The "Produce Exchange" is in its infancy, but for the same period of time since its organization, the association has shown more vitality than did the Board of Trade in its early years. Its government and its future permanency, is in the hands of men of large experience in this line of industry, who we doubt not will prove themselves tobe as wise and sagacious as were those who thirty years ago first laid the foundation of the Board of Trade. And that Chicago will regard the association with equal pride—Mr. D. Richards who was chosen President, at the annual meeting held in the month of May, 1878, is a gentleman most favorably known, having been engaged for the past twenty years in this city as dealer in Butter and Cheese, and so extensive has his business been, that he is not only known throughout our own country, but is equally as well known in Europe. Many years ago, when western butter was far inferior to the quality that comes from our creameries to-day, Mr. Richards was engaged in shipping to Europe grease butter, which was used for greasing sheep in the highlands of Scotland. This grade of butter was the only one that was permitted to land free of duty on the shores of the "tight little island;" better qualities of butter was charged 20 per cent. duty.   And the inspectors in those days, so as to avoid, imposition being practiced upon the revenue laws, when butter was received at the Custom House, resorted to the practice of steeping a rod or stick into hot tar, and then run it through the packages so as to make it grease butter whether it was or not.   In subsequent years Mr. Richards has been one of the principal packers and shippers of fine grades, and of second quality of butter suitable for the table, as also for bakers use, for which there was always a large demand.   But the West, always progressive, takes precedence in the quality of her Butter over all other sections, the yield of her creameries are now regarded in New York as in all other markets as superior to any butter no matter from whence it comes.   Mr. Richards with his long experience still continues to make a specialty of butter and cheese—is engaged in shipping to all points, mostly in car lots.   He is regarded as one of the very best judges of butter in the country.   He was selected by the butter dealers as one of the judges, in connection with Captain Hunter, of the firm of Hunter, Walton & Co. of New York city, a well known expert, at the "Fair" held at Uhlich's Hall, in the winter of 1877.   At which place he demonstrated the superiority of his judgment by marking on the same line of butters which had been selected by Eastern experts.

FRUIT AND BERRY ORDINANCE OF THE CITY OF CHICAGO.

We copy the following from the minutes of a meeting of the members of the Produce Exchange:

The vexed question as to the size and style of the fruit package to be hereafter used in this market seems to have been practically settled at last by the joint action of the Produce Exchange and the city authorities. The former organization recently passed the following preambles and resolutions by an almost unanimous vote:

"WHEREAS, The question of packages of fruit has been for the past two years thoroughly agitated in both city and country, to such an extent in the city that the City Government felt compelled to pass ordinances last season in relation thereto, and in many country places dealers in small fruits are compelled to empty out of boxes and measure up by the quart to satisfy their customers, and,

WHEREAS, Although the city authorities have been defeated before the courts on the ordinances passed last season, they still propose to pass such ordinances as will stand the test of the law; and,

WHEREAS, If such ordinances should be of a condemnatory nature by inspectors appointed by the city authorities, which is not improbable, it would lead to great annoyance and loss to the shippers; and,

WHEREAS, Manufacturers have not yet made the packages for the coming season's fruit, nor have the growers yet bought them; and,

WHEREAS, We fully believe it is for the interest of the fruit trade generally, and each individual shipper as well, to have all fruits put up in full-sized packages, and to be of good uniform quality, be it

Resolved, That we, the fruit commission men of Chicago, assembled, do strongly and unqualifiedly recommend to all our shippers that they use for all small fruits the full quart-box of sixty-seven cubic inches, we fully believing that it can be used for transportation as well as anything smaller, except for red raspberries, and for them we as strongly urge full pint. We most heartily condemn the "so-called" one-third quart box, or the use of pint boxes for anything except red raspberries. For all Southern fruits, such as peaches, pears, etc., we recommend the continuance in use of the third-bushel box as being the best. For Michigan fruits of similar kinds we cannot too strongly urge the use of the full-peck basket only. It is sma'l enough for any trade, and if the fruit is of uniform quality through the basket no one can complain. Whortle or blueberries come to our market in all sizes of boxes and drawers. The least we can recommend our shippers is to measure the packages fairly and mark the number of quarts contained in such package plainly. It causes you but little trouble, and saves us a great deal of guessing, and our customers from a great deal of fault-finding.

Resolved, That in the shipment of fresh vegetables, that which purports to be a bushel-box shall hold a bushel; much fault has been found with these packages the past season.

Resolved, That a barrel of apples shall be three bushels. The barrel certainly should not be less than a full-sized flour barrel.

Resolved, That in the future in making and quoting the market, the price shall be given on full measure packages. Short measure will be sold in proportion. In other words we do not expect to get any more than its proportionate value for any fruit packed in less than the full-sized package.

Resolved, That we have no doubt but that the Common Counsel of Chicago will pass further ordinances on this question ; and if they should be of a condemnatory nature, the only thing we could do would be to send you the inspector's certificate in place of an account of sales.

Resolved, That we do not countenance any deception in quantity or quality of fruit, either in original packages or re-packed here.

Resolved, That we extend the hand of cordial fellow-ship to all of the shippers that in the past have used the full-sized package and taken pains to properly pack their fruit. We know it has paid you better to do it, it pays us better to handle it, and pays the consumer that uses it, and we hope the coming season will see it the rule, and not the exception.

The following resolution was also adopted and a committee appointed :

Resolved, That the Chair be authorized to appoint a committee of five, to confer with the City Law Department and the Judiciary Committee of the Council in regard to the differences that do exist, and that may arise between the wholesale fruit dealers, and the city authorities.

The City Counsel on Monday evening, February 18th, 1878, adopted the following Ordinance on the same subject, which has received the Mayor's signature and thus become a law :

Be it ordained, etc. : SECTION 1. All fruits and berries sold or offered for sale within the City of Chicago to consumers or to retail dealers within the said city shall be sold and offered for sale only by barrel, bushel, or some aliquot part of a bushel, according to the table of dry measure, or in packages which contain in full measure a barrel, a bushel, or some aliquot part of a bushel, according to the table of dry measures, or by the pound: *Provided*, that for fruits the package known to the Chicago market as a third of a bushel box may also be used ; and *provided further*, that this section shall not apply to dry, preserved, or pickled fruits or berries, or to the sale of fruits retailed at a fixed price per piece or number.

SEC. 2. All fruits and berries, fresh or dried, sold or offered for sale in the city of Chicago in packages shall be substantially of equal goodness in every part of the package; any package of fruit packed so as to be in violation of this section shall be subject to seizure and condemnation by the health officers of the city as deleterious to public health.

SEC. 3. Any person who shall sell or offer for sale by the package within the city of Chicago any fruit or berries in packages not of the size and description required by the first section of this ordinance, or who shall sell or offer for sale any fruit or berries in packages the contents of which are not substantially of equal goodness throughout the package, contrary to the second section of this ordinance, shall, upon conviction, be fined not less than $5 nor more than $25 for every such violation.

SEC. 4. The ordinance entitled "An ordinance to regulate the selling of fruits, berries, etc.," passed May 21, 1877, approved May 24, 1877, is hereby repealed.

SEC. 5. This ordinance shall be in force from and after its passage.

It is earnestly hoped that country growers and shippers will cheerfully accept the situation, and in buying their berry baskets will take care that they are of full quart capacity, and their peach baskets full pecks. Any other course must result in great annoyance to the trade, and loss to the shipper as well. The state of public feeling, and the attitude of the city authorities, is such that the quart box and peck basket will be the measure of value, and boxes and baskets not up to this standard will be discriminated against, and will only be salable at much lower prices than the full measure. Hence it is for the interest of every grower to take immediate steps to fully comply with the law. There is no doubt that every shipper will receive as much for his crop under the new system as he did under the old."

By order of the Directors.

JOHN E. COWLES, Secretary.

Game Law of Illinois.

Section 1. Be it enacted by the people of the State of Illinois, represented in the General Assembly: That it shall be unlawful for any person or persons to hunt or pursue, kill or trap, net or snare, or attempt to kill, trap, net or snare or otherwise destroy any wild buck, doe or fawn, wild turkey, prairie hen or chicken, ruffed grouse (commonly called partridge or pheasant), between the first day of January and the fifteenth day of August in each and every year; or any quail between the first day of January and the first day of October in each and every year; or any woodcock between the first day of January and the first day of July of each and every year; or any wild goose, duck, Wilson snipe, brant, or other water-fowl between the fifteenth day of April and the fifteenth day of August in each and every year; and every person so offending shall, for each and every offense, be deemed guilty of a misdemeanor, and on conviction shall be fined in any sum not less than ten dollars, nor more than twenty-five dollars and costs of suit, and shall stand committed to the county jail until said fine is paid; provided that such imprisonment shall not exceed ten days.

Sections 2, 3, 4 and 5 not of special interest to merchants.

Sec. 6. No person or persons shall sell or expose for sale, or have in his or their possession for the purpose of selling or exposing for sale, any of the animals, wild fowl or birds mentioned in Section 1 of this act, after the expiration of thirty days next succeeding the first day of the period in which it shall be unlawful to kill, trap, or ensnare such animals, wild fowl or birds, and any person so offending shall, on conviction, be fined and dealt with as specified in Section 1 of this act.

Sec. 7. The provisions of this act shall not be construed as applicable to any Express Company or common carrier into whose possession any of the animals, wild fowl or birds herein mentioned shall come in the regular course of their business, for transportation, whilst they are in transit through this State from any place without this State where the killing of such animals, wild fowl or birds shall be lawful. But, notwithstanding, the having or being in possession of any such animals, wild fowl or birds as are mentioned in Section 1, upon any of the days upon which the killing, entrapping, ensnaring, netting, buying, selling, or having in possession any such animals, wild fowl or birds, shall be unlawful by the provisions of this act, shall be deemed and taken as "prima facie" evidence that the same was ensnared, trapped, netted or killed in violation of this act.

Instructions for Packing Butter.

We wish to impress upon the minds of Western dairy-men and makers of butter the necessity of paying strict attention to this great interest, which is yearly growing in magnitude, if they wish to compete with other sections. The packing and package used are almost as essential points as making, and this fact should be remembered. Of course, all packages of butter are not alike, and cannot all be sold at the same price, but a little more care and attention paid in this respect—packing —would do considerable towards bringing about more uniformity in prices. Very often commission merchants receive complaints from country shippers, stating that their butter was as good as their neighbors', which was sold as choice, and probably 2@5c. higher than theirs. This may be so in their estimation, but other parties may differ; their neighbors' butter may have been put up in more desirable packages—probably new tubs—while theirs was packed in jars or old tubs. Then, again, their butter may have been streaked—probably only the least trifle, while their friends' may have been straight and uniform in color—all which would naturally tend at times to make a wide difference in price and create dissatisfaction. Parties should be careful and pack butter uniform in color, and should particularly remember the fact that streaked lots— no matter how sweet and choice—cannot be brought in competition with lots running uniform in color; the latter always commanding a much quicker sale at a fair premium, and in every way compensating dealers for their extra labor and care. Another fault is that a large portion of the butter during hot weather turns sour and rancid very suddenly sometimes before being received, although it may have left in good and sweet condition from whence it was sent. This fault lies in the power of makers to remedy to some extent. For instance, the cream may have stood too long, or not worked sufficiently to take out all the buttermilk, while another fault would be in not salting properly. These minor points, although but trifling at first, are more noticeable after they have gone through first hands and finally reach other markets. The packing and packages used are, however, of no secondary account in the matter of realizing the best market prices, and during hot weather particularly should shippers be especially careful in regard to packages. Jars and pails should be avoided as much as possible, the former costing more freight, besides being a package not easily handled. In handling at the stations and express offices, and even in forwarding, jars and pails are often placed on top of each other, and as there are no covers for protection, the quality is materially damaged by defacement, and the price is considerably lessened. Tubs and firkins should be used exclusively, but in tubs some discrimination is made. The New York ash tub is taken in preference to others on account of its neater appearance, though some parties use home-made tubs, which they claim answers their purpose. Another reason why these tubs are becoming more in favor on the part of dealers is the fact that they sell more readily to shippers, and parties can also more readily agree on tare if a certain make and tub is used to which they are accustomed. Therefore tubs and firkins are recommended to be the most desirable, and in the end the most economical packages used. In packing parties should be careful to soak their packages well before using. In making always use the best salt—Higgins' Factory-filled Dairy is most generally used. Parties should be careful to pack their butter solid, completely filling the packages, and spread a piece of clean, new bleached cotton cloth over it, dipped in brine, neatly tucked in at the edges, so when removed it will not damage appearance. Another fact which we wish to call the attention of farmers and makers of butter to is that they should buy their own packages and pack their own butter in original packages, so as to do away with this country second-handed repacking business, which causes so much streaked butter.

Advice to Shippers of Butter.

Commission merchants complain that considerable " made-over " butter is being consigned to this market, the bulk of which they find very difficult to sell, and in most cases can only be disposed of at a loss to the shipper. This is not, of course, applicable to all " made-over " butter that is received from the country, but more particularly that from country store-keepers, who think that by a certain patent process, and the use of patent machinery and by coloring, they can turn common and fair grades of butter into A No. 1 quality. To those who are not versed in the business and do not give it their sole attention, let this bit of advice suffice—" let well enough alone "—for by endeavoring to re-work a fair lot of solid butter for the purpose of improving the quality by the aid of machinery and coloring, they generally make a failure of it, and when it is sold here will only command low-grade prices. A good quality of solid butter, no matter if not particularly straight and uniform in color, can, if sweet, be sold to the local retail trade; but after going through this patent process and coloring up, it is generally refused by this class of buyers, while shippers and re-packers refuse to buy, excepting at low-grade prices, as it is not worked to their satisfaction, and they prefer to do their own re-packing. A practice prevails in the country of re-packing common and good qualities; country dealers thinking that by working the two grades into one they can sell the entire lot for a good price. In this they are mistaken, as dealers here know the difference between a good and a poor quality. Hence the best policy is to ship butter to this market just as it is received at country points, and in most cases the result will be more satisfactory to both the shipper and the commission merchant. It is not the fault of the merchant here if he cannot sell this re-worked stock at prices to let out the country shipper, although countrymen generally lay the blame to them, and considerable dissatisfaction naturally results from this source.

Roll Butter.

Care should be taken in packing and shipping; country shippers and dealers are in the practice of sending roll butter to this market in every conceivable package, including barrels, pine boxes, etc. The above-named packages should be entirely avoided, as pine will have a tendency to affect and flavor the butter, while barrels are too large, and not easily handled, besides the weight crushes the rolls. New tubs or hardwood boxes are the most desirable, while half barrels or kegs will do equally as well, and these only should be used. Care should also be taken before putting the butter in packages, that all the sides and ends of the package be lined with new, white muslin, thus keeping the butter from defacement by touching the wood. Another bad practice is in putting the butter up in paper; this should not be done, as the paper sticks to the butter and damages the appearance. Each roll should be separately placed in a piece of new muslin cloth, washed in warm water to take out the starch, and thoroughly wet in good brine. The rolls should also be of uniform color, not packing the light and fresh made with other that has been colored.

Tare on Butter Packages.

Some dissatisfaction is expressed by parties in the country in regard to the tare allowed by commission merchants on butter packages. This fault of improper tare, if there is any, is not the fault of the merchant here, but that of the country dealers in not allowing for sufficient soakage. The tub most in use at present is the ash tub, which parties allow to soak, say from four to five days in brine, but after the butter has been packed these packages absorb sufficient to make the packages weigh fully one-half to one pound more. The lightest ash tubs, containing 60 to 65 pounds of butter, weigh, when dry, about $7\frac{1}{2}$ pounds, and when thoroughly soaked from $9\frac{1}{2}$ to 10 pounds, while the heavy ash tubs, which contain 60 to 65 pounds of butter when dry, weigh about $9\frac{1}{2}$ to 10 pounds, and when soaked 12 pounds.

Country dealers also complain that their gross weight does not hold out full, but that there is more or less shrinkage. This the country dealers can remedy by not putting so large a quantity of salt and brine on their butter. It is impossible for commission merchants to sell salt or brine for butter, and in nine cases out of ten the salt has to be taken off and the brine let out before a sale can be made. A little caution in this respect will bring about a better understanding between country shippers and commission merchants.

Instructions to Shippers.

Shippers of produce would do well to carefully observe the following instructions, which will be advantageous to both the shipper and commission merchant.

All articles should be packed in clean packages, and care should be taken to pack articles as neatly as possible.

Articles which are sold by weight should have the gross and tare marked plainly on each package, and those sold by count should have the number.

In shipping dressed poultry and game, mark each package with the various kinds and amount contained in each package.

The address of the commission merchant should be marked plainly with marking-ink on each package, also from whom consigned; nail or tack an invoice on each package, and also send an invoice by mail.

Country shippers should also make it their aim to send none but choice articles to this market, if they wish to obtain ready sales. Poor lots, not fit for use, and such which country shippers would not use themselves—they being good judges—should not be sent here to trouble and pester our merchants.

Game for Shipment.

Pack solid without gutting in layers, in boxes or barrels, smoothing each bird down nicely; use neat packages; put your count on each barrel or box.

Woodcock and snipe should never be gutted, and woodcock need heavy icing.

Bear should be shipped whole carcass, and gutted.

Deer in carcass, always gutted, and leave horns on; but when skinned, hind quarters or saddle, wrap up in clean white cloth, or skin out the fore quarters and fold back the skin over the hind quarters and tie up.

Antelope only pays to ship hind quarters, wrapped up in whole hide.

Elk and buffalo, only ship hams cut from the calf; the but and heavy cow are not worth shipping; wrap up in clean white cloth. Rabbits, never gut or skin.

Mountain sheep, ship whole carcass gutted, not skinned, leaving horns on.

Wild pigeons, dressed should not be gutted, but if crop is full should be pulled off with the head and neck, and the wings chopped off close, or leave one joint. Feathered wild pigeons, pull the tail feathers and chop off the wings; in warm or doubtful weather both must be well iced between each or alternate layer of birds; use tight packages.

Live pigeons should have a supply of corn, well soaked, placed in their coops, if coming any distance, and coops should have two bars on top of each coop lengthwise, to keep them, when piled on top of one another, at least three inches apart, to prevent suffocation; not over fifty or sixty birds in a coop.

How to Kill and Ship Poultry.

Poultry should never be killed by the wringing of the neck, but should be killed by bleeding, by means of opening of the veins, or by cutting off the head, so as to let them bleed freely. If the latter be done, care should taken and draw the skin over the neck and tie secure before shipping. Deface the neck as little as possible, as the looks will materially aid in bringing outside prices. Poultry should be picked dry, which can easily be done by plucking before the bodies are cold, which always give poultry a nice appearance. However, when scalded, the water should be as near boiling as possible, and yet not really boil. The poultry should be dipped, so that the water will have proper effect on the skin, and penetrate the feathers. The feathers should be picked immediately, but care should be taken and not break the skin. Do not remove the entrails. Poultry, before being killed, should be kept twenty-four hours without food; full crops injure the appearance, and are liable to sour, by which the sale would be greatly injured. Before packing it should get thoroughly dry and cold, but not frozen. Moderate-sized boxes should be used, but avoid very large packages as much as possible, as there is considerable trouble in handling, besides being more difficult to sell. In packing use clean boxes, and line the ends and sides with paper. Always pack as closely as possible, and fill the boxes well, so there will be no chance for the poultry to move about.

To Shippers of Cheese.

Factorymen and shippers of cheese should be more particular in regard to the size of the boxes in which they ship cheese. The boxes should not be higher than the actual height of the cheese, as the heat during warm weather causes them to puff and swell in the vacant space, which naturally damages the sale.

To Shippers of Vegetables.

Country shippers have found fault with the returns commission merchants make of green peas and other green vegetables sold by the measure, they claiming that sales for full amounts are not returned. Country shippers should bear in mind that in transportation vegetables become more or less heated and packed, and lots invariably run short when sold.

Instructions for Preserving Eggs.

To make pickle, use stone lime, fine salt, and water in the following proportions : 1 bushel of lime, 8 quarts of salt, 25 tin-quart pails of water.

The lime must be of the finest quality, free from sand and dirt—lime that will slack white, fine and clean. Have the salt clean and the water pure and sweet, free from all vegetable or decomposed matter.

Slack the lime with a portion of the water, then add the balance of the water and the salt. Stir well, three or four times, at intervals, and then let it stand until well settled and cold. Either dip or draw off the clear pickle into the cask or vat, in which it is intended to preserve the eggs. When the cask or vat is filled to a depth of fifteen or eigthteen inches, begin to put in the eggs, and when they lay, say about one foot deep, spread around over them some pickle that is a little milky in appearance, made so by stirring up some of the very light lime, particles that settle last, and continue doing this, as each foot of eggs is added. The object of this, is to have the fine lime particles drawn into the pores of the shells, as they will be by a kind of inductive process and thereby completely seal the eggs. Care should be taken not to get too much of the lime in, that is, not enough to settle and stick to the shell of the eggs and render them difficult to clean, when taken out. I believe that the chief cause of thin, watery whites in limed eggs; is that they are not properly sealed, in the manner described ; of course another cause is, the putting into the pickle, old stale eggs, that have thin, weak whites. When the eggs are within about four inches of the top of the cask or vat, cover them with factory cloth and spread on two or three inches of the lime that settles in making the pickle, and it is of the greatest importance that the pickle is kept continually up over this lime. A tin basin, holding about six to eight dozen eggs, punched quite full of inch holes, edge muffled with leather and a suitable handle, about three feet long, attached, will be found convenient for putting the eggs into the pickle. Fill the basin with eggs, put both under the pickle and turn the eggs out ; they will go to the bottom without breaking.

When the time comes to market the eggs, they must be taken out of the pickle, cleaned, dried and packed. To clean them, secure half of a molasses hogshead, or something like it, filling the same about half full of water. Have a sufficient number of crates of the right size, to hold 20 or 25 dozen eggs, made of laths or other slats placed about three quarters of an inch apart. Sink one of these crates in the half hogshead, take the basin used to put the eggs into the pickle, dip ihe eggs out and turn them into this crate. When full, rinse the eggs by raising it up and down in the water, and if necessary to properly clean them, set the crate up and douse water over the eggs, then if any eggs are found when packing that the lime has not been fully removed from, they should be laid out and all the lime cleaned off before packing. When the eggs are carefully washed, as before described, they can be set up or out in a suitable place to dry—in the crates. They should dry quickly and be packed as soon as dry. In packing, the same rules should be observed as in packing fresh eggs. Vats built in a cellar, around the walls with about half their depth below the cellar surface, about four or five feet deep six feet long and four feet wide, are usually considered best for preserving eggs in, although many use and prefer large tubs made of wood.

The place in which the vats are built or the tubs kept should be clean and sweet, free from all bad odors, and where a steady low temperature can be maintained ; the lower the better, that is down to any point above freezing. Besides the foregoing, other methods for preserving eggs have been devised, such as varnishing, greasing, oiling and rolling in flour, but these methods will only answer in a small way, for an individual's private use, it being nearly or quite as much as the eggs are worth to put them in merchantable shape ; in fact, it is nearly impossible to do so, as the shells will never look uniformly clean. Several processes have been patented and sold to a considerable extent, but the old liming process undoubtedly stands ahead up to the present time.

Instructions for Packing Eggs.

Use none but new packages, and these of uniform size and appearance, containing the same number of dozen, the same number of layers, and the same number of eggs in each corresponding layer ; to secure bright, dry, clean straw, free from must, a season in advance ; to have it cut with a first-class cutting machine that is kept perfectly sharp, so that the packing will be crisp and elastic, made so by cutting the straw clean off without mashing, as is the case when cut in a poor machine with dull knives. The importance of good packing would be better appreciated by shippers, if they could see their consignees selling the eggs. When the head is taken out of a barrel, properly packed with crisp elastic straw the head springs up, and the eggs show up in good condition. But the removal of the head from a barrel packed with musty, mashed straw, scares the customers; then if the packing has sagged down, leaving room for the eggs to shift, and the top layer from careless heading has a number of broken eggs that have matted the straw, the customer thinks the whole barrel is in the same condition, and not only refuses to buy that barrel, but looks with suspicion on that brand.

The eggs in each barrel should be of uniform quality as far as freshness and cleanliness are concerned. If a shipper has stale or dirty eggs and wants to ship them he should put them up in separate packages with a distinct mark. The regular brand should be uniform in every respect in order to secure and maintain a reputation ; all doubtful eggs should be sorted out and marked with the outside brand.

Dealers should employ none but good, careful packers, those who take a pride in doing their work well. The one who does the heading, should be a man with good judgment, a careful painstaking man, who will do his work without breaking the eggs on the top layer, and at the same time secure them against shifting. Too much care cannot be taken in this part of the work, because nothing injures a brand more than broken eggs on the top layer.

What Constitutes a Car-Load.

Salt, brls	70
Lime, brls	70
Flour, brls	90
" Sacks	200
Whisky, brls	60
Softwood, cords	6
Cattle, head	20
Hogs, head	60
Sheep	100
Apples, bu	360
Sweet Potatoes, bu	360
Split boards, ft	9,000
Flooring, ft	13,000
Siding	17,000
Shingles	40,000
Wheat, bu	340
Corn, "	300
Oats, "	680
Barley, "	400
Flax seed, bu	360
Irish Potatoes, bu	430
Bran, bu	1,000

COMMISSION CHARGES FOR SELLING MERCHANDISE.

	Option Car Lots.	Com. Car Lots.	From Store.
Wheat	½ ct. per bu.	1 ct. per bu.	
Corn	" "	" "	
Oats	" "	" "	
Rye	" "	" "	
Barley	" "	" "	
Hops		2½ per ct.	5 per ct.
Seeds		" "	" "
Broom Corn		" "	" "
Cured Meats	1 per ct.	1 per ct.	" "
Beef			" "
Pork	1 per ct.	1 per ct.	" "
Dressed Hogs	½ " "	1¼ " "	3 per ct.
Live Hogs		$6 per car	
Cattle		50c. per head	
Sheep		$6 per car	
Dressed Sheep			5 per ct.
Butter		2½ per ct.	" "
Lard	2½ per ct.	1 per ct.	" "
Tallow		2½ per ct.	" "
Hides		" "	" "
Wool		" "	" "
Lumber		" "	
Shingles		" "	
Lath		" "	
Beeswax			5 per ct.
Beans		2½ per ct.	" "
Green Fruits		5 "	10 per ct.
Dried Fruits		2½ "	5 "
Foreign Fruits		5 "	10 "
Cheese		2½ "	5 "
Eggs		" "	5 "

Game		5 to 10 "
Hay ard Straw	$5 per car	
Potatoes	5 per ct.	10 per ct.
Potatoes, Sweet	" "	10 "
Poultry, Live		5 "
Poultry, Dressed		5 "
Vegetables		10 "
Veal		5 "
Furs		5 "
Feathers		5 "
Cider	5 per ct.	10 "
Dried Peas		5 "
Honey		5 "
Nuts, Domestic		5 "
Nuts, Foreign		5 "
Fish		5 "

SHIPPING PERISHABLE MERCHANDISE,

BY THE

Tiffany Summer and Winter Cars.

In this era of wonderful and eminently practical inventions and discoveries in the domain of science, there is nothing in which more marked advancement has been made than in the direction of providing means for the transportation in a fresh, sound condition of the perishable products of the sea, the soil, the dairy, and the packing house. By the invention and perfection of refrigerator cars, refrigerator storehouses, and refrigerator steamers, the commerce of the world has been facilitated and promoted beyond anything like approximate computation, and what a few years ago was an absolute impossibility has thereby been rendered easy of accomplishment.

We can to-day receive luscious fruits, berries, and vegetables of California, Florida, Texas and other remote sections in as fresh condition as when they were gathered. During the hottest weather of summer Wisconsin creamery butter is laid down in the New York market in better condition than that of the Westchester dairyman living ten miles from the city. In the shops of England, France, and Germany, American dressed beef is sold as fresh and sweet as where it was slaughtered —yes, in even improved condition, on account of the age it has gained in transit. By reason of these modern transportation and preserving facilities, tropical and semi-tropical fruits, which would otherwise not pay for the labor employed in gathering them, are freighted thousands of miles to a ready and remunerative market. By the same means dairy products are carried to points where they command double or treble the price which could be realized where they were produced. The same with reference to fresh meat, poultry, eggs, fish, and other perishable property. Thus the surplus products of one section are made to supply the wants of another and distant region, to the encouragement and promotion of local industries and the enrichment of the people. That these commercial conveniences for the exchange and marketing of the respect-

WINTER AND SUMMER CARS. 141

ive products of different countries and climes are the means of saving
millions of dollars annually is unquestionable.

Desiring to give information with regard to this important and interesting matter to the producer and shipper of such commodities, we have
obtained the following information from Mr. Charles F. Pierce, Manager
of the Tiffany Refrigerator Car Company, at his office, 74 Washington
street, to wit: That the Tiffany Summer and Winter Cars and Chill
Rooms had proved a perfect success, and the numerous testimonials in
his possession from railroad corpora·ions, commission firms, shippers and
receivers fully corroborate his statements. These cars and storehouses
are constructed on strictly scientific principles, and the results of their
thorough test and use during the two years in which they have been
operated are of the most satisfactory character. The outside jacket se-
cures perfect insulation, protecting the contents from all atmospheric
conditions and changes, whether of heat or cold, thus insuring the great
desideratum—an equable temperature in all latitudes. This important
advantage has been demonstrated in a multitude of cases, as, for instance,
in the transportation, in summer, of dressed beef from Denver to Philadelphia, 2,400 miles, through four extreme climatic changes, the trip oc-
cupying 14 days, and the beef reaching its destination in perfect order.
A Philadelphia commission firm report receipts of California fruits
shipped in Tiffany cars as opening up "in splendid order," and express
the hope that all fruit shipped to them will come in these cars, "as it has
always been a great difficulty to have the fruit arrive in good order."

A prominent fruit firm in this city say, the Tiffany car "has proved
itself a success for the transportation of California fruit to Chicago and
the Eastern cities. With outside temperature of 110 degrees in the
shade, the car maintained an even temperature, with small consumption
of ice."

This Company now have 95 cars running in all parts of the country,
and 7 in Europe, and will add to the number as rapidly as possible. They
are employed on many of the principal railway lines, and bid fair to
supersede all other cars for the carriage of perishable merchandise.

The Atlantic Coast Line has adopted the Tiffany transfer car for the
transportation of strawberries and early vegetables from Charleston to
New York, having met with signal success therewith last season. These
small cars measure 8 feet in length by 7 feet in height, and four of them
can be carried on an ordinary platform car, allowing of their being transferred to boats or vessels with the utmost facility. The Company will

build this winter for the same Line 50 more of their small and 12 of their large cars. On the opening of the projected steamship line between Galveston and Vera Cruz, it is proposed to employ these transfer cars for the transportation of the delicious fruits of Mexico to Chicago, which can be done in a week's time, and the fruits laid down here without the slightest deterioration in freshness or flavor. Our people can then indulge in tropical luxuries in midwinter, at prices which will bring them within the reach of all.

The Tiffany cold storage rooms have been erected at several shipping points in Texas, Florida, and other parts of the South, wherein are placed fruits, etc., intended for Northern markets and allowed to remain until their temperature is reduced to the proper degree for safe shipment in the refrigerator cars. In testimony to the efficacy of this system, the officers of the Pomological Association of Texas say : " We take great pleasure in certifying that we have carefully examined the system of Cold Storage and Refrigeration adopted and practiced by the Tiffany Refrigerator Car Company, and which is now in operation at their Houston Chill Rooms, and have also eaten of the fruit kept in said house for a week and over, and are fully satisfied that all perishable fruits and vegetables can be preserved and marketed in good condition to Northern cities whenever the system is properly applied." By this means the mammoth and luscious strawberries grown in that State can be placed on the Chicago market early in March and profitably sold at 25 cents per quart.

Foreign communities having become fully convinced of the feasibility of importing American fresh meats—a trade, by the way, which is assuming gigantic proportions—these refrigerator warehouses have been built at Paris and Vienna, and are to be erected in Russia and other European countries. Thus are the advantages and economics of refrigeration, as perfected and utilized under the universally approved Tiffany system, benefiting incalculably the nations of the world.

DECISIONS IN ADMIRALTY.

By Robert Ray, Chicago Bar.

COLLISION.

Even flagrant fault committed by one of two vessels approaching each other from opposite directions, does not excuse the other from adopting every proper precaution required by the special circumstances of the case to prevent a collision. Damages equally divided in a case of collision on an application of this rule. *The Maria Martin*, 12 Wal. 31.

A vessel racing in order to enter a harbor before another, and pre-occupy a loading place, condemned for a collision resulting. *The Spray*, 12 Wal. 366.

When a vessel is sailing in close proximity to other vessels, the fact that her hands are engaged in reefing her main sail, is no sufficient ex-cuse for failure to keep a lookout, or to take such precautions as are needful to avoid collisions. *Thorp* v. *Hammond*, 12 Wal. 408.

If a vessel at anchor in a gale could avoid a collision threatened by another vessel, and does not adopt the means for doing so, she is a participant in the wrong, and must divide the loss with the other vessel. *The Sapphire*, 11 Wal. 164.

A schooner meeting a steamer, approaching her on a parallel line, with the difference of half a point in the courses of the two, held a col-lision case upon evidence to have kept on her course, and therein to have done what she ought to have done. *The Fannie*, 11 Wal. 238.

A steamer approaching a sailing vessel, is bound to keep out of her way, and to allow her a free and unobstructed passage. Whatever is necessary for this, it is her duty to do and to avoid whatever obstructs or en-dangers the sailing vessel in her course. The obligation resting on the sailing vessel is passive rather than active, the duty to keep on her course. If, therefore, the sailing vessel does not change her course so as to embarrass a steamer, and render it impossible or at least difficult for her to avoid a collision, the steamer alone is answerable for the damages of a collision if there is one. *The Fannie*, 11 Wal. 238.

On crowded waters and powerful vessels, lookouts are bound to sleepless vigilance and indefatigable care. *The Adriratic*, 13 Wal. 475.

The absence of a proper lookout unimportant, when the absence of one has nothing to do with causing the disaster. *The Fannie*, 11 Wal. 238.

A steamer crossing another so as to involve risk of collision condemned; 1st, for not keeping clear, having the other on her starboard; 2d, being the following vessel. *The Columbia*, 10 Wal. 246.

The rule of navigation which requires a special lookout, does not apply to a case where the absence of a lookout had nothing to do in causing the collision or loss. *The Farragut*, 10 Wal. 334.

One vessel meeting another of a foreign nation on the high seas, is bound to observe towards her the rules of navigation prescribed by the municipal laws of the country of the former. *The Scotia*, 3 Chicago Legal News, 10.

Where two sailing vessels are beating in the same direction, the hindmost vessel is bound to know that the leading vessel must come about on running out of her course, and the time and place when and where such manœuver must take place, and she must take proper measures to permit the movement without coming into dangerous proximity. *The Nellie D.*, 5 Bl. C. C. 245.

Sailing ships are "meeting end on," within the meaning of the 11th article of the Act 29th April, 1864 (2 Bright Dig. 428), when they are approaching each other from opposite directions, or on such parallel lines as involve risk of collision on account of their proximity, and when they have advanced so near to each other that the necessity for precaution to prevent such a disaster begins. *The Nichols*, 7. Wal. 656; *The Dexter*, 23 Wal. 70.

The expression "meeting *nearly* end on," in the same act, includes cases where two sailing ships are approaching from nearly opposite directions, or on lines of approach substantially parallel, and so near to each other as to involve risk of collision. *The Nichols*, 7 Wal. 656.

A sailing vessel discovering the lights of a steamer nearly ahead on a dark and cloudy night, has no right afterwards to change her course, on the idea that she has not been seen by the steamer. *The Scotia*, 5 Bl. C. C. 227; *The Alhambra*, 2 Ben. 158.

Under the Act of 29th April, 1864, it is the duty of a steamer, which, when crossing so as to involve the risk of collision, has the approaching vessel on her own starboard side, to keep out of the way of such approaching vessel, and the duty of the steamer so approaching to keep her course. *The Chesapeake*, 1 Ben. 23.

A steam vessel in a fog must reduce her rate of speed to a moderate one or abide the consequences, unless some special reason be shown for maintaining the rate adopted. *The D. S. Gregory*, 2 Ben. 166.

When a steamer proceeding in the dark, hears a hail before her from some source which she cannot or does not see, it is her duty instantly to reverse her engine, not merely to "slow." *The Hypodame*, 6 Wal. 216.

Although it may be true, as a general rule, that a free steamer meeting a tug incumbered by tows must keep out of the way, it does not follow that the tug can monopolize the channel, or disregard the rules of navigation. *Hern v. The Anthracite*, 2 Leg. & Ind. Rep. 58.

A ship navigated in a peculiar manner, which has the effect of incapacitating her for the time from moving out of the way so as to avoid collision, does so at her own risk, and will be held answerable for the damage done by a collision resulting from such incapacity. *The Hope*, 2 W. Rob. 8.

The rule that all steamers bound up or down the river with vessels in tow, should keep as near the right hand shore as their respective drafts of water will permit, is a just and proper one. *Hern v. Anthracite*, 2 Leg. & Ind. Rep. 58.

Though a tug may be unable to stop the tow attached to her, and that duty be cast on the incumbered boat, yet this inability will not justify the tug in disregarding the rule of porting her helm and keeping to the starboard side of the river. *Hern v. Anthracite*, 2 Leg. & Ind. Rep. 58.

A vessel meeting a tug and tow in a narrow passage, having been previously signalled to keep to the right, is not excused from the consequences of a collision, by the fact that she could not take the right of the channel without grounding. 9. Wal. 522.

A vessel in tow is not, therefore, excused from keeping close watch and observing and obeying all signals. *Northern Transportation Co.* v. *The Maria Martin*, 1 Chic. Leg. News, 57.

Inevitable accident, as respects a colliding vessel, means that such vessel has endeavored by every means in her power, with due care and caution, and a proper display of nautical skill, to prevent the collision. *The Baltic*, 2 Ben. 452.

Mistakes committed in moments of impending peril by a vessel, in order to avoid a collision, made imminent by the mismanagement of those in charge of another vessel, do not give the latter, if sunk and lost, a claim on the former for any damages. *The Nichols*, 7 Wal. 651.

The mere fact that a vessel is sunk by a collision, is not of itself sufficient to show that the loss was total, nor to justify an abandonment. *The Baltimore*, 8 Wal. 377.

Where a vessel at anchor is struck by one in motion, the presumption of law is that the collision is caused by the negligence of the latter, unless the former were anchored in an improper place. *The Beaver*, 2 Ben. 118.

If a vessel be anchored at a place forbidden by the regulations of the port, she will be held to have contributed to a collision, and liable to a proportion of the damages. *The Baltic*, 2 Ben. 396.

When a tugboat is injured by a collision, the proper inqiury is as to what she could have been chartered for per day in the business of towing (during the time she was laid up for repairs), regard being had to the market price. *The Maybey*, 4 Bl. C. C. 439.

The fact that the claimant, by putting repairs on the libellant's vessel, suit brought, made her worth more than before the collision, is no bar to a recovery for demurrage for the time occupied in making such repairs. *The Santee*, 6 Bl. C. C. 1.

A steam tugboat is not responsible for an accident to her tow by running upon a rock not generally known. *The Angelina Corning*, 1 Ben. 109.

COMMON CARRIER.

The term "dangers of lake navigation," include the peril which arises from shallowness of the waters at the entrance of the lake harbors. *Transportation Co. v. Donner*, 11 Wal. 129.

MASTER.

As between the owners and the master, nothing more is required of the latter than the exercise of such care, diligence and skill, as the duties of his position demand. 9 Wal. 370.

The master can be superseded in his command whilst at sea only as a last resort in a case of the utmost emergency. *The Anastasia*, 1 Ben. 166.

The master cannot bind the cargo for extraordinary expenses in towing his vessel into port, without resorting to every ordinary means of repairing the damage sustained in a gale, so as to enable her to reach port under sail. *Lyon* v. 928 *Bbls. Salt*, 2 Chic. Leg. News, 317.

If the situation of the master be such that he cannot communicate with the owners, he may sell a portion of the cargo in order to raise means to make necessary repairs to the ship. *The Star of Hope*, 9 Wal. 203.

The master is not liable for injuries to cargo caused by unloading and reloading, in order to pass a bar; it is the duty of the mate to see to the loading. *Nupham* v. *Biessel*, 9 Wal. 370.

The power of the master to make contracts about his vessel in the home port of the owners is limited. *The Tribune*, 3 Sum. 144.

The master cannot, by signing a false bill of lading for cargo not actually shipped, charge the vessel or the owner, who is not a party to the fraud. *The Freeman* v. *Buckingham*, 18 H. 182.

The master is clothed with the power to decide, from the facts before him, whether a jettison be necessary for the common safety. *Laurence* v. *Minturn*, 17 H. 100.

If the master act with reasonable prudence, according to his best judgment, he is not responsible for the consequences. *The Gentlemen*, 1 Bl. C. C. 196.

In cases of necessity the master is the agent of all concerned, and his acts, in the exercise of a sound discretion, are binding on all parties in interest. *Miston* v. *Lord*, 1 Bl. C. C. 355.

LIEN FOR FREIGHT.

The lien for freight under a charter party attaches as soon as the cargo is put on board. *The Hermitage*, 4 Bl. C. C. 474.

A carrier may, if he see fit, deliver a part of a particular shipment without impairing his right to hold the residue for the freight upon the whole consignment from which the part so detained was taken. *Sears* v. *Bags of Linseed*, 1 Cliff. 68.

The lien for freight is inseparably associated with the possession of the goods, and is lost by an unconditional delivery. *Wills* v. *Sears*, 1 Bl. 108.

But there may be a conditional delivery to the consignee, with an understanding that the lien for freight shall not be affected. *Wills* v. *Sears*, 1 Bl. 108.

Shipowners, as a general rule, have a lien upon the cargo for freight, but it may be modified or displaced either by direct words or by stipulations incompatible with the existence of such a right.

A bill of exchange or note given for a precedent debt, does not extinguish the debt unless such was the agreement of the parties. A bill or note falling due before the unloading of the cargo, and protested and unpaid is no discharge of the lien; and the shipowner in such a case may stand upon it as fully as if the acceptance had never been given. *The Bird of Paradise*, 5 Wal. 545.

A conditional and qualified delivery does not discharge the lien for freight, such as a delivery with the understanding that the freight is to be paid when it is completed. *Guughum* v. *Tons of Coal*, 4 Bl. C. C. 368.

LIEN FOR WAGES.

The master's agreement in a foreign port to raise the wages of the seamen, will not give them a lien for such increase prior to that of creditors for advances to the ship. *Sears* v. *Bags of Linseed*, 1 Cliff. 68.

A claim for wages after twenty-one months continuous service, is not deemed a stale one where there has been no change of ownership. *Fisher* v. *The G. C. Morris*, 27 Leg. Int. 204.

The master sailing the vessel on shares, under an agreement to man and victual her at his own expense, does not affect the seaman's lien for wages. *Fisher* v. *The G. C Morris*, 27 Leg. Int. 204.

FREIGHT.

The rights of shipowners to freight depend on the bills of lading, and are not affected by the terms of the charter party. *Wills* v. *Sears*, 1 Bl. 108.

The assignee of the bill of lading who receives the goods is bound to pay the freight, except under special circumstances. *Trask* v. *Duvall*, 4 W. C. C. 181.

If a vessel put back to her port of shipment in distress, and the cargo be there sold and the proceeds received by the shipper, no freight is due. *Miston* v. *Lord*, 1 Bl. C. C. 354.

The right to freight earned upon the homeward voyage follows the ownership of the vessel. *The Henry*, 1 Bl. & H. 465.

Freight contracted for in gross, for a voyage out and home, cannot be apportioned, unless under special circumstances. *Weston* v. *Minot*, 3 W. & M. 457.

The crew are not authorized to make a jettison of any part of the cargo in case of distress without order of the master. *The Nimrod*, Ware 1.

An Outline of the Evidence of General Average.

BY ROBERT RAE, Chicago Bar.

1. General, gross or extraordinary average means a contribution made by all the parties concerned towards a loss sustained by some of the parties in interest for the benefit of all; and it is called general or gross average, because it falls upon the gross amount of ship, cargo and freight.

2. In the United States, partial loss and average are understood by commercial men to mean the same thing, and average other than general, includes every loss for which the underwriter is liable, except general average and total loss. *Wadsworth* v. *Pacific In. Co.*, 4 Wend. 33.

3. General average is incurred where the expenses or losses arise in a case of emergency, not produced by the misconduct or unskilfulness of the master, and not resulting from the ordinary circumstances of the voyage. *Ross* v. *Ship Active*, 2 Wash. C. C. 226.

4. It is also true that in order to make a case of general average, it is necessary not only that the ship should be in distress and the property endangered, and a part sacrificed in order to preserve the rest, but it is necessary also that this sacrifice should be voluntary.

5. The property sacrificed for the benefit of other property must be embarked in a common adventure. If A's vessel is about to come in collision with B's, which is at anchor, and B cuts his cable and thus avoids it, he has no claim for contribution against A for the loss of the cable or anchor.—*The John Perkins*, 21 L. Rep. 87, 97.

6. The sacrifice must be with the intention of saving the remaining property, and must be successful. *Williams* v. *Suffolk Ins. Co.*, 3 Sum. 513. *Scudd* v. *Bradford*, 14 Peck. 13. *McPerson* v. *Tyson*, 8 Mass. 467.

7. The most usual form of this voluntary sacrifice, which is the foundation of general average, was a "jettison" of cargo to lighten the ship; therefore, if no possibility of saving the ship, thereby there is no contribution in nature of general average. *Crockett* v. *Dodge*, 3 Fairf. 190.

8. Goods laden on deck of sailing ship and jettisoned, do not as a rule make a cause for general average. *Ray* v. *Milwaukee Belle*, 18 Am. L. R. 311.

9. But if there be a usage for their being so carried, it is otherwise, and they make a case for general average. *Toledo Co.* v. *Spears*, 16 Ind. 52.

10. So, if the goods be carried on the deck of a propeller or steamboat. *Gillett* v. *Ellis*, 11 Ill. 579. *Harris* v. *Moody*, 4 Bosw. 210. Confirmed on appeal, 30 N. Y. 266.

11. The word "jettison" not only applies to the cargo, but also to masts and anchors cut away, or sails and rigging cast off to save the ship from wreck. *Walker* v. *U. S. Ins. Co.*, 11 S. & R. 61.

12. The right to contribution (general average) does not depend on any real or presumed intention to destroy the thing cast away, but on the fact that it has been selected to suffer alone, and thus avert the common peril. *Sturgis* v. *Cary*, 2 Curt. C. C. 59.

13. If a mast be broken, and for the safety of the ship it be found necessary to complete the fracture and cast the mast with sails and rigging into the sea, this would form a case of general average, the amount of loss to be estimated at the value of the mast at the time it was cut away, not the price which a new mast would cost. *Teetsman* v. *Clamageran*, 2 La. 195.

14. Where cargo is exposed by shipping in lighters or otherwise for the general benefit, and damaged, the loss is a subject of general average, as the damage was a direct consequence of such exposure. *Lewis* v. *Williams*, 1 Hall, 430, 451.

15. The same rule is applicable when masts are cut away for general preservation of vessel, and corn was thereby damaged by water, the cutting away being the *indirect* cause of damage. *Cagrath* v. *Church*, 1 Carnes, 196.

WHAT EXPENSES COME INTO GENERAL AVERAGE.

Expenses of entering or quitting a port of distress to refit, and of discharging and reloading cargo there, including warehouse rent, pilotage, towage, port charges, etc., as also accidental damage done to cargo in consequence of unloading.

Wages and provisions of master and mariners from time vessel bears away from course of her voyage to a port of refuge, to the time she is again ready for sea.

Disbursements made for the common benefit, whether the ship and cargo be eventually saved or not. *Spafford* v. *Dodge*, 14 Mass. 66.

Expenses of detention while frozen up in a port put into by the master voluntarily for repairs.

Ransom paid to a captor whether piratical or belligerent for the benefit of all concerned. *Douglas* v. *Moody*, 9 Mass. 548. *Lawson* v *Hall*, 4 Dall. 459.

Expenses of delay and making claim for vessel and cargo in case of capture. *Speyer* v. *New York Ins. Co.*, 3 Johns, 88. *Dorr* v. *Union. Ins. Co.*, 8 Mass, R. 494.

Salvage in case of capture. *Williams* v. *Suffolk Ins Co.*, 3 Sumner's R., 270 and 510.

Expenses of remunerating salvage services rendered for the common safety in case of shipwreck.

Commissions and interest on advances for general average purposes.

Commissions collecting general average. *Barnard* v. *Adams*, 10 Howard, 270.

Expenses of surveys and of discharging cargo, either to cool it, or in order to extricate ship from perilous situation—as to float a stranded ship. This includes the hire of lighters in some cases to avoid landing cargo when impracticable.

Expenses incurred to restore cargo when shifted by perils of the sea.

Expenses of unloading part of cargo for purpose of ship getting into port of destination, owing to some *unusual* and *unforeseen* obstruction.

Temporary repairs to ship made at an intermediate port, for the purpose of prosecuting the voyage and of no peculiar benefit to shipowner.

Ship's provisions consumed by workmen from the shore employed in repairing, and by wreckers.

Expenses landing cargo when vessel goes into a port of refuge, so long as to be under the control of the master, and the voyage be not abandoned. *Nelson* v. *Belmont*, 5 Duer. 310.

Expenses of shipping or hiring an anchor and chain after a chain has parted, or the costs of an unsuitable anchor and chain supplied under like circumstances.

Freight lost by jettison of goods. *Nelson* v. *Belmont*, 5 Duer. 310-322.

CONTRIBUTING INTERESTS.

The value of the ship for contribution is her worth to her owners in the state in which she arrives.

In case of *voluntary stranding*, the measure of loss is the value at the time when the ship was run aground.

The value of the *cargo* for contribution is what it has produced or would produce at, as nearly as possible, the time of its arrival, stripped of freight duty and landing charges, the portion of the cargo jettisoned to be estimated in like manner, and added to net value of cargo saved.

All property on board vessel at time of jettison and saved, unless attached to person of passengers, is to be brought into contribution. *Harris* v. *Moody*, 3 New York Reps.

The value of *freight* for contribution is the net freight on the goods saved and carried, deducting crew's wages, port charges, etc.

ADJUSTMENT.

The proper time and place for adjusting a general average loss is on the arrival of the ship at her port of destination.

D. RICHARDS,

FORMERLY RICHARDS & GOOCH.

Commission Merchant,

Produce and Provision Broker,

BUTTER & CHEESE A SPECIALTY,

3 LaSALLE ST., COR. S. WATER,

CHICAGO.

Orders and Correspondence Solicited.